PRIVATIZATION OF PUBLIC ENTERPRISES IN LATIN AMERICA

PRIVATIZATION OF PUBLIC ENTERPRISES IN LATIN AMERICA

Edited by William Glade

A Copublication of the International Center for Economic Growth,
the Institute of the Americas, and
the Center for U.S.–Mexican Studies

ICS PRESS
San Francisco, California

Inquiries, book orders, and catalogue requests should be addressed to ICS Press, 243 Kearny Street, San Francisco, California, 94108. Telephone: (415) 981-5353; FAX: (415) 986-4878.

Cover design by Sarah Levin.

Cover illustration by David Diaz.

Index compiled by Shirley Kessel.

Distributed to the trade by
National Book Network, Lanham, Maryland.

Library of Congress Cataloging-in-Publication Data

Privatization of public enterprises in Latin America / edited by
   William Glade.
         p.   cm.
   "A copublication of the International Center for Economic
Growth, the Institute of the Americas, and the Center for
U.S.-Mexican Studies."
   Includes bibliographical references and index.
   ISBN 1-55815-128-1 (paper)
   1. Privatization—Latin America. 2. Government business
enterprises—Latin America. I. Glade, William E.
HD4010.5.P76   1990
338.98—dc20   90-15584
                                                           CIP

Contents

List of Abbreviations

AFP	Administradora de Fondos de Pensiones
AHMSA	Altos Hornos de México
AID	Agency for International Development (United States)
BANADE	Banco Nacional de Desarrollo (Argentina)
BANCOMEXT	Banco Nacional de Comercio Exterior (Mexico)
BANJIDAL	Banco Nacional de Crédito Ejidal (Mexico)
BNDES	Banco Nacional de Desenvolvimento Econômico e Social (Brazil)
CAP	Compañía de Acero del Pacífico (Chile)
CBC	Companhia Brasileira de Cobre (Brazil)
CCB	Companhia Celulose da Bahia (Brazil)
CCE	Consejo Coordinador Empresarial (Mexico)
CCT	Compañía Chilena Tabacos (Chile)
CDE	Corporación Dominicana de Electricidad (Dominican Republic)
CEA	Consejo Estatal del Azúcar (Dominican Republic)

CED	Centro de Estudios para el Desarrollo (Chile)
CEIM	Compañía Exportadora Importadora de Maíz (Mexico)
CELPAG	Companhia Guatapará de Papel e Celulose (Brazil)
CFE	Comisión Federal de Electricidad (Mexico)
CGT	Confederación General del Trabajo (Argentina)
CHILECTRA	Compañía Chilena de Electricidad (Chile)
CHILGENER	Compañía Chilena de Generación Eléctrica (Chile)
CHILQUINTA	Compañía Chilena de Electricidad de la Quinta Región (Chile)
COBRA	Computadores e Sistemas Brasileiros, S.A. (Brazil)
CODELCO	Corporación Nacional del Cobre de Chile (Chile)
CONASUPO	Compañía Nacional de Subsistencias Populares (Mexico)
CORDE	Corporación Dominicana de Empresas Estatales (Dominican Republic)
CORFO	Corporación de Fomento de la Producción (Chile)
COSINOR	Companhia Siderúrgica de Nordeste (Brazil)
CTC	Compañía de Teléfonos de Chile (Chile)
CVRD	Companhia Vale do Rio Doce (Brazil)
DEP	Holding Company for Enterprises (Argentina)
ECLA	Economic Commission for Latin America (United Nations)
ECOM	Empresa Chilena de Computación e Informática (Chile)
ELECTROBRAS	Centrais Elétricas Brasileiras (Brazil)
ELMA	Empresa Línea Marítimas Argentinas (Argentina)
EMBRAER	Empresa Brasileira Aeronáutica (Brazil)
EMBRATEL	Empresa Brasileira de Telecomunicações (Brazil)
EMEC	Empresa Eléctrica de Atacama (Chile)
EMEL	Empresa Electricidad Limari (Chile)
EMELAT	Empresa Eléctrica de Coquimbo (Chile)
ENAEX	Empresa Nacional de Explosivos (Chile)
ENAP	Empresa Nacional de Petróleo (Chile)
ENDESA	Empresa Nacional de Electricidad (Chile)
ENTEL	Empresa Nacional de Telecomunicaciones (Argentina)

FFCC	Ferrocarriles (Mexico)
FLACSO	Facultad Latinoamericana de Ciencias Sociales (Chile)
GDP	Gross domestic product
GNP	Gross national product
IADB	Inter-American Development Bank
IANSA	Industria Azucarera Nacional (Chile)
IMF	International Monetary Fund
ISCOTT	Iron and Steel Company of Trinidad and Tobago
MAFERSA	Material Ferroviaria, S.A. (Brazil)
NAFINSA	Nacional Financiera (Mexico)
OPEC	Organization of Petroleum Exporting Countries
PEMEX	Petróleos Mexicanos (Mexico)
PETROBRAS	Petróleo Brasileiro (Brazil)
PIRE	Programa Immediato de Reconstrucción Económica (Mexico)
PSBR	Public sector borrowing requirement
SAS	Scandinavian Airlines
SEGBA	Servicios Eléctricos del Gran Buenos Aires (Argentina)
SIBRA	Eletrosiderúrgica Brasileira (Brazil)
SOQUIMICH	Sociedad Química y Minera de Chile (Chile)
TNC	Transnational corporation
USIMEC	Usiminas Mecânica (Brazil)
YPF	Yacimientos Petrolíferos Fiscales (Argentina)

Preface

Privatization, or the turning over of some government enterprises and activities to private investors, has become a key part of Latin America's drive for modernization and revived growth in the last decade of the twentieth century. Latin American governments have come to realize that they have had too large a role in the production of goods and services.

When governments try to do what the private sector can do as well or better, the state's managerial and financial resources are diverted from essential services that only the state can provide equitably to all its citizens—education, public health, and roads, among others. As Mexico's President Carlos Salinas de Gortari has pointed out, privatization is thus not necessarily a conservative's dream of shrunken government, but rather a neoliberal conception of government concentrating on what only it can do, thus doing it better. As William Glade persuasively argues in his conclusion to this volume, privatization is most successful as part of a broad program of structural reform to infuse the whole economy with competitive market forces—a set of reforms that much of Latin America now sees as a key for its economic revival and long-term growth.

With the exception of Chile, Latin American governments began the privatization process slowly and selectively, with relatively minor

enterprises targeted for transfer to the private sector. In recent years, however, these governments have become increasingly committed to accelerating and broadening privatization, both as a matter of preference and as
a response to fiscal realities. Labor conflicts in state-owned enterprises,
inability to gain more substantial relief from the external debt service
burden, the need to reduce inflationary government deficits by eliminating subsidies to unprofitable state-owned enterprises, the need to generate significant new resources to attack the massive "social deficit"
resulting from nearly a decade of economic crisis and austerity budgets,
and the huge capital investment needs of even profitable state-owned
enterprises that are urgently in need of technological modernization—all
played a part in the intensification of government efforts to privatize.
Opinion polls showing broad public support for the policy—in Mexico,
even for reprivatization of the banking system—undoubtedly encouraged governments to proceed.

Accordingly, the terms of the debate over privatization in Latin America have shifted dramatically. Increasingly, the issue is no longer *whether* to
privatize, or even *what* to privatize, but *when* and on *what terms*—selling
price, foreign or domestic buyers, buyers' commitments to invest in modernization, and so forth. Nevertheless, important questions remain unan-
swered about the feasibility of large-scale privatization programs under
prevailing international market conditions and about their effects on income distribution and sectoral concentration of capital in the long term.

Privatization of state-owned enterprises is an experiment-in-progress
on a global scale, and only through systematic comparative analysis can
the strengths, limitations, and long-term consequences of this policy be
fully understood. In planning the May 1988 conference from which this
book resulted, the Center for U.S.–Mexican Studies and the Institute of the
Americas thus felt a need to examine a wide range of experiences in Latin
America as well as in Western Europe. This volume takes a reflective,
in-depth look at early experiences with privatization in six Latin American countries. The lessons drawn by the Latin American authors of these
case studies and editor William Glade constitute a valuable guide to the
opportunities and pitfalls in Latin America's next phase of privatization
and structural reform processes, now gaining increased momentum and
political support throughout Latin America.

Nicolás Ardito-Barletta	Paul H. Boeker	Wayne Cornelius
General Director	President	Director
International Center for	Institute of the	Center for U.S.–
Economic Growth	Americas	Mexican Studies
		University of
		California, San Diego

January 1991

Acknowledgments

This book and the conference from which it evolved were made possible by grants from the following institutions: the Ford Foundation, the Tinker Foundation, the William and Flora Hewlett Foundation, the Howard Heinz Endowment, and the Center for Iberian and Latin American Studies at the University of California, San Diego. The editor also gratefully acknowledges other forms of support received from the Woodrow Wilson International Center for Scholars, the Commission for the Study of International Migration and Cooperative Economic Development, and the Program on U.S.–Mexican Relations of the Johnson School of Public Affairs at the University of Texas.

CHAPTER 1

The Contexts of Privatization

It is ironic that most of the privatization around the globe is being managed by the public sector. Seldom has it been contemplated that the privatization process itself might be privatized—that private initiative might hunt out and bid for potentially profitable investment opportunities within the ample confines of the state sector. Instead, the initiative in starting such programs, the selection of what is to be privatized, and much of the follow-up come from official agencies, aided in some instances by government-sponsored contractors and consultants.

Privatization holds special appeal in the United States, and it is the U.S. government's Agency for International Development (AID) and its client organizations that have become the policy's standard-bearers in third world countries—joined now, at a discreet distance, by the World Bank, the International Monetary Fund (IMF), and, more remotely, the Inter-American Development Bank. Like a school of fish, these national and multinational public sector institutions, and the dependent private organizations they have spawned, roam the world. The objects of their search are beleaguered governments that might prove susceptible to the financial inducements they offer for governmentally engineered change.

Privatization strategies have thus far been driven chiefly by other concerns of public policy. Foremost among these are the twin needs born of balance-of-payments difficulties: to consolidate the financial position of the public sector and to improve competitiveness of the economy. The logic of privatization stems from a larger set of policies that promote structural adjustments to give less-developed and newly industrialized economies a better shot at making their way in the world economy. Privatization looks particularly attractive in the light of today's protracted crisis brought on by excessive external debt. Governments have also felt the need to get the parastatal sector in hand so that by lowering public sector borrowing they may arrest inflation, irrespective of the level of external indebtedness. More generally, the process responds to new policy imperatives originating in the restructuring of production patterns that has taken place in the world economy over the past several years.

The Setting for Privatization

There was an isolated round of privatization in the 1960s, when Argentina returned the faltering surface transport system of metropolitan Buenos Aires to private ownership. During the same period, two state petroleum companies, Petróleos Mexicanos (PEMEX) in Mexico and the Yacimientos Petrolíferos Fiscales (YPF) in Argentina, allowed private drilling contractors to operate in the petroleum industry. Nevertheless, the movement toward privatization did not really take hold until the 1970s. In fact, the policy previously prevailing in Latin America had been to increase state control. There, the panoply of regulation was extended and the number and size of state-owned enterprises grew steadily from the 1930s through the 1970s.

The initial impetus for spreading statism was the need to cope with the Great Depression, when capitalism's future looked bleak in many parts of the world. By the close of the 1930s, the dislocations of World War II occasioned the continuation and elaboration of state interventionism, adding weight to the already visible impulse to use state power to fashion a more industrialized economy and internalize the growth dynamic. Neither of the growth stimuli that had propelled Latin America forward since the nineteenth century—export expansion and foreign investment—seemed a reliable prop for economic development. Even in the most advanced economies, Keynesianism seemed to promise a permanently enlarged economic role for the state where social democratic policies had not already carried the entrepreneurial state still farther afield.

In the aftermath of the war, the pioneering policy theory of the United Nations Economic Commission for Latin America (ECLA) accorded the state additional economic functions, at a time when development theory was still in its infancy and there were no well-established rivals to ECLA's policy prescriptions. To be sure, development advisers from the United States and the World Bank were more market oriented in their recommendations. But neither of these alternative sources had a more elaborated and venerable doctrine to offer—nor, for that matter, any long track record in underdeveloped areas on which to argue a claim of superiority. Taking the lead among its sister regional agencies, ECLA seized the high ground in the theoretical dispute and parlayed its institutional lead into a preeminent position as the formulator of development strategies from the perspective of the underdeveloped countries themselves. In an era of burgeoning nationalism, this particular form of product differentiation proved extraordinarily successful in securing buyer attachment on the part of public officials who were shopping for policies with which to chart the future.

While ECLA was coming into its own as the policy mentor for a region, and even before, expansion of public sector involvement in industrial, financial, and commercial undertakings was creating an articulate and well-placed segment of society. This "state bourgeoisie" found in ECLA's policy package a rationale for its own growth and sense of public mission. What is more, surrounding the proliferating parastatal companies were groups that had a vested interest in their operations: organized workers on payrolls that often paid little heed to redundancy, industrial and household consumers of the parastatals' frequently subsidized output (including borrowers with access to concessionary credit dispensed by government-owned banks), and supplier firms who profited handsomely from what, in effect, were captive markets. These were later joined by the partners in joint ventures with the state, who benefited from special fiscal treatment and other favors, and by the politically influential promoters of business ventures who could secure bailouts from state financial intermediaries when their investments, often financed with state credits or state-guaranteed loans, turned sour. Foreign-owned companies also profited from the protection accorded their manufactures during this period.

Considering the multitude of factors that supported the prevailing interventionist regime, it is not surprising that by the 1970s Latin America had become one of the regions most characterized by state economic guidance. Hence, when the Organization of Petroleum Exporting Countries (OPEC) oil shocks and accumulating petrodollars impelled bankers to look abroad more vigorously for clients, Latin American government agencies were able to fund a mountain of seemingly plausible investment projects, while the parastatals were lining up at the loan window to cash in on their perceived status as preferred borrowers. The ballooning of the foreign debt was, therefore, largely attributable to the region's development strategy.

Compounding the problem was the fact that the parastatal sector had, in most cases, outrun the existing capacity for legislative or executive branch oversight. Exempt from the discipline of the market, the parastatals were often exempt from the discipline of public authority as well, although they could count on sovereign authority to back their creditworthiness in the international capital market.

While this scenario of state-led growth was unfolding in the 1970s, questions surfaced about its viability for the future. The Mexican business community, not noted for its fondness for economic liberalism, first evinced a mounting unease over the untrammeled expansion of the state during the Echeverría administration (1970–1976). Contemporaneously in Brazil, no less statist in its policy style than Mexico, Congress made a first stab at imposing a surveillance scheme on the parastatals. There, too, the business community expressed its first serious doubts about the extent of "statization" in the economy.

It was in Chile and Argentina, however, that these concerns were first translated into policy. In Chile, privatization simply could not be dodged when the government that in 1973 replaced the statist Allende regime faced an immediate need to revive the production system. The situation closely resembled the circumstances that drove the government of the Soviet Union toward its New Economic Policy to repair the damage of wartime communism.

Three years later, the Argentine military, in the characteristically irresolute way economic policy has been implemented in that country, also turned to privatization. They began with a divestiture of once-private firms that the state had acquired through receivership operations.[1]

A Preview of Findings

What lessons can be derived from the varied experiences of the six countries selected for study? A full account is given in the concluding chapter of this volume, but a quick look ahead at the outset may provide a useful orientation. The first lesson concerns the critical role of policy sequencing.

Nothing serves more effectively as a prelude to privatization than establishing a general policy framework to correct the larger distortions of resource allocation. Fiscal restraint and cautious monetary policy to stabilize the price system seem to serve as the best point of departure, for with these the government begins to level the playing field. These actions create a decision-making environment in which all managers, whether in the private or parastatal sector, can begin to make systematic plans. Bringing the exchange rate into a realistic alignment is no less essential for its bearing on the whole structure of relative prices.

Two further steps are required to pave the way for privatization if one hopes to strengthen allocational efficiency in the economy. The first is to introduce a trade liberalization that reduces the distortions born of trade policy and pressures all firms producing traded goods—whether the firms are public or private—to make more efficient use of the resources they deploy. The second is to scale down, and eventually eliminate, subsidies to the parastatal sector, an objective that fiscal restraint should set in motion. This, too, is necessary to establish the price structure as a meaningful guide to resource allocation and to force parastatal managers to behave like managers in the private sector. These changes do not necessarily require deregulation. In some fields, where contestable markets are not present, as in the so-called natural monopolies, new regulation may have to be devised and imposed as a surrogate for the market.

Privatization, or reprivatization, need not await the completion of these reforms, provided that their implementation is sufficiently certain to influence expectations. But in general, the larger the enterprise to be privatized, the more judgments are likely to be colored—in the absence of clear market-favoring policies and policy expectations—by opportunities for rent seeking or by uncertainty. Further, spreading exposure to the discipline of the market is likely to curtail labor opposition to privatization when it is eventually introduced.

Although it could be argued that the foregoing measures are sufficient to induce market-constrained behavior and therefore satisfy the requirements for efficient allocation, the experience of the countries studied suggests at least two more policy desiderata. On the one hand, the process of privatization is not without cost, so institutional mechanisms that reduce transaction costs and capture the benefits of learning-by-doing are far preferable to a dispersed procedure that distributes responsibility for privatization too widely and maximizes the opportunities for institutional resistance. Vesting major responsibility in a lead institution that commands the expertise needed to manage privatization is, thus, ordinarily a crucial strategic measure. On the other hand, although privatization is normally associated with deregulation, and properly so in many instances, the Latin American experience also suggests the importance of re-regulating. New regulations may be required to strengthen the operation of the capital market, to forestall the emergence of undue concentrations of economic power in the private sector, and to install an appropriate operating framework for public utility industries.

A Preview of Country Experiences

Of the countries covered in this collection, Chile came first to privatization. It did so not so much for ideological reasons as from a practical necessity to use reprivatization to revive the economy after the debacle of the early 1970s. It also had a longer-term objective: to revamp an economy that had come to be perceived as an underachiever in the postwar expansion of the global economy and a weak performer alongside more energetic economies elsewhere in Latin America. The contrast with other economies in the region was especially galling in view of Chile's long history of orderly civilian government, its favorable resource endowment, and a population that was better educated than the regional average. To be sure, the military and their technocratic advisers draped an ideological mantle over the ensemble of policies—trade liberalization, fiscal restraint, and decontrol of prices. This made the enterprise respectable to some, but anathema to others. Yet the ideological trappings of market economics and the neoclassical paradigm had, after all, been around a very long time without attracting many followers. The interesting question, therefore, is why Chile should finally embrace privatization when the policy tradition of the country had been so different for decades. A case can be made that this development was much less attributable to political motivation than to the suspension of routine politics that allowed technocratic considerations to come to the fore.

The Chilean case is interesting for other reasons as well. As the earliest of the privatization experiments—barring some earlier random episodes such as the hugely successful privatization of urban transport in Buenos Aires during the 1960s—the Chilean experience is the one that is not debt driven. Since the inception of the program predated the problems of Latin America in the 1980s, when so many policy objectives were swamped by the imperatives of debt management, it reveals with particular clarity the complementarity of privatization with an array of other policy goals. For the same reason, as a pioneering venture that has now gone on for a decade and a half, it provides a remarkably instructive picture of the process of learning-by-doing by which economists set such store these days (faith in theoretical constructs having long since been fine tuned away). The privatization strategies now in use differ considerably from those employed at the outset of the free-market experiment, for they have been consciously modified to deal with problems encountered in the program's earlier years.

On the one hand, the evolutionary character of privatization policy renders less interesting the whole matter of ideology, which on a grand scale functions more or less as a presumed constant. Sovietologists, for example, years ago learned to deemphasize ideology as a factor useful for understanding the dynamics of most centrally planned economies. Only in a few historical instances—such as China's Cultural Revolution and the Stalinist collectivization of agriculture or Fidel Castro's more recent neo-Albanian proclivities—does ideology seem to carry much explanatory power when it comes to dealing with the workings of economic systems. Hence, we can, and should, profit from the experience of scholars of Soviet-style systems by not letting ideological window dressing cloud the determining variables of policy formation and economic performance in Chile, though this is not to dismiss the possible relevance of ideology for other social science concerns.

On the other hand, the comprehensiveness of the Chilean reform and its subsequent pragmatic adaptation serve to highlight the pitfalls of privatization policies that are incomplete in conception and application. In Chile, as in most other Latin American countries in this century, the standard policy mix included, until quite recently, state-led growth and a panoply of interventionist measures that served mainly to socialize losses and privatize gains. There, as elsewhere, the interpenetration of the public and private sectors was such that real progress in allocational efficiency was possible only after an understanding was reached on the fundamental relation between macroeconomic policies and microeconomic attainments. Reform of the former, in other words, was necessary if reforms of the latter were to succeed. Put succinctly, the success of programs to privatize the public sector depended in large measure on the success of programs to privatize the private sector, releasing it from its multiple moorings in a morass of state-sanctioned privilege and favor. After some major blunders, the policy makers of Santiago finally achieved this insight, with paradoxical consequences. Chile is the country with the longest and most comprehensive commitment to privatization. While implementing this policy, it made substantial headway in putting its economic house in order, thereby preparing the way to regain full access to the international capital market and restoring its capacity to grow. Consequently, it alone of the countries discussed in this volume is now in the position to mount a large, multiyear investment program on behalf of its public enterprises.

In contrast, nowhere are the pitfalls posed by the complex web of interests that built up around the interventionist tradition more plainly illustrated than in Argentina. After a considerable amount of reprivatization in the late 1970s, the Argentine program came to a halt in the 1980s. It was not just a result of the ambivalence of the Radical party toward privatization. Nor could it be ascribed to the role of Peronism as an insistent presence in national political life, though only lately have leaders of the Justicialist party come round to a tepid endorsement of privatization. Spirited opposition has all along come from both public sector and other trade unions affiliated with the powerful Confederación General del Trabajo (CGT), Latin America's most substantial labor movement and the mainstay of the Justicialist rank and file. In this guise, a threat from the Peronist camp has hovered over the scene since the restoration of competitive civilian politics, dampening publicly declared support for privatization in the long run-up to the 1989 elections.

No less a problem, however, has been the country's notoriously unresponsive bureaucracy, including public enterprise managers and directors. This group has parlayed divisions in the body politic and the weakness of civil society into an organizational inertia that favors maintaining the status quo ante. They have been joined by a motley assortment of allies that includes the businesses that supply the parastatals. The Argentine state is not a strong one, but it is sprawling. In the context of a fragmented electorate and stalemated politics, the bureaucracy is able to influence the outcome of events more than one might think—particularly when the privatization process has been structured as cumbersomely and opaquely as it has in Argentina. The cavalier disregard for established procedural guidelines that has been displayed by the Ministry of Public Works and Services in handling the privatization cases of Aerolíneas Argentinas and the national long-distance communications company, Empresa Nacional de Telecommunicaciones (ENTEL), indicates how obtrusive political criteria can still be in economic life along the Río de la Plata.

The case for preeminence of the political is especially strong when so much of the private sector appears historically wedded to an intricate scheme of rent-seeking behavior, in which business profits derive not from innovation and production efficiency but from such things as the manipulation of returns on capital by government regulation, favoritism in government spending, and preferential tax treatment. In the depression of investment options that has plagued Argentina almost steadily since the onset of the Great Depression, the main chance for gain—indeed the essence of firm-level survival strategies—has most often come from proximity to the public treasury, to the spending power of the parastatal sector, and to the decisional processes whereby public authorities wield regulatory power over a myriad of economic relations. Access, not competitive prowess in production, has been the most treasured asset. And transparency is perceived more as letting the cat out of the bag than as the sine qua non of allocational efficiency. On both counts, social efficiency criteria have had a way of falling into the shadow of private reckonings, while de facto "private" decisions are lodged in the nether reaches of the bureaucracy.

There is, of course, a very large latent constituency for privatization: consumers who must endure deficient public services. Some of these, such as the firms in the Buenos Aires financial district, even studied the possibility of setting up their own local telephone exchange, equipped with the advanced technology needed for transmitting information quickly and reliably. The effort was quashed by the state to preserve the monopoly of ENTEL, with which the Ministry of Public Works and Services was promoting a joint venture with the Spanish telephone company (a mixed enterprise). Notwithstanding the legal problems raised by the choice of the Spanish partner through negotiation rather than the prescribed open bidding and congressional approval, and despite objections that Telefónica de España was not the best choice for providing the desperately needed upgrading of technology, the government persisted in its course of action. Politicians argued that a Spanish company would not be perceived as an imperialist threat; doubtless there was also a desire to repay a large political debt owed the Spanish government for its backing of the Alfonsín administration. Projects to establish other local-service telephone companies (as municipal, regional, cooperative, or private enterprises) met a similar fate, and proposals to privatize gas distribution through local companies also failed to receive government support. In short, in Argentina as elsewhere, the difficulty of transforming the consuming public into an organized constituency for the general interest has allowed organized special interest groups to preempt the policy process and claim the day.[2]

The lingering enforced austerity of today's restructuring programs seems scarcely calculated to detach beneficiaries of state favor from their customary preferences, given the paucity of attractive investment options. At least this is not likely until state spending has completely dried up. The controlled spread of competition implied by the Argentine-Brazilian integration program may eventually help straighten things out, assuming, of course, that this program does not fall prey to the Byzantine processes of policy making that have undone many other stabs at economic rectification in Argentina. Meanwhile, the problems the IMF encountered in getting Argentina to conform to its conditionality requirements indicate that this particular kind of institutional transformation is no easy matter. Despite prodding from multilateral institutions, in mid-1989 state-owned companies still accounted for about half of the country's gross national product (GNP), and government subsidies made up 30 percent of the budgets of the 117 state-run industries.

The Mexican case replicates, albeit more opaquely still, some of the institutional features of the Argentine situation. In Mexico, however, it seems less a question of political stalemate (or of political indecision, as in Brazil) than defensive maneuvering on the part of an embattled political party under unprecedented attack for its very real accomplishments in reorganizing policy, as well as for its shortcomings and for circumstances over which no government could gain control. In Mexico, quite as much as anywhere else, the interrelation of political and economic equilibrium stands out in bold relief—even if the decisional mechanisms by which that joint equilibrium has been historically maintained have been shrouded in fog. In the Mexican setting, structure seems unmistakably related to function, as sociologists have long taught, but the ways in which this has been so are, to say the least, elusive—never more so than in the organizational shell game through which the privatization program has been announced and carried out.

Two metaphors come to mind as a means of grasping the poetics of Mexican politics: one applicable to the state as it operates in relation to its citizenry; the other, to the state as seen from the outside. For the former, the privatization program thus far is very much like Salome and her seven veils, with just enough being revealed at each drop to interest major onlookers in the electorate (and among the country's foreign creditors) in a continuation of the performance—but with enough remaining veiled to preserve the attractiveness of the political class in its seductive routines. Indeed, even the term remains under wraps; the government carefully avoids "privatization" and speaks instead of "disincorporation." Whether the artistry of the act will prove sufficient to achieve its intended goal—electoral victories and debt relief—remains to be seen. For the time being, the government has continued the performance with remarkable grace, given the tilt of the stage on which it has been dancing and the irregular syncopation of the tune.

In Mexico, as in Argentina, protracted economic troubles have compounded problems by creating an environment that is essentially inhospitable to energetic privatization in its usual guises. The anemic private sector investment capacity and weakened market incentives (as far as the internal market is concerned) have strengthened the attachment to such state favors as remain available amid the general liberalization of trade. Supposedly, the constriction of aggregate demand would also enhance the relative appeal of export markets, but reaching these effectively requires considerable product and organizational adaptation, along with new investments to facilitate both. It is precisely this that has been made almost unattainable by the acute shortage of capital occasioned by financial repression and crowding out. Under the circumstances, both the interest in purchasing state assets that are put on the block and the ability to acquire them are diminished, especially considering that mismanagement and austerity have combined to decapitalize

many of these state-owned firms. Potential buyers face substantial reha-
bilitating investments to make privatized companies viable. At the same
time, the enthusiasm for rationalization of parastatal management, with
the elimination of rent-seeking opportunities this entails, has diminished as well.

Nowhere is this predicament likely to be more inimical to long-run
allocational efficiency than in the pressure that reforms already enacted
have placed on the government to preserve its capacity to distribute
political favors through parastatal operations. These favors include rationing credit through the nationalized banking system in a market
under severe stress from a still large public sector borrowing requirement. It could reasonably be argued, though, that the private sector has
a genuine interest in improved parastatal management precisely in
order to relieve congestion in the capital market. Nonetheless, this pos-
its again the familiar problem of trade-offs between a generalized long-
term benefit and immediate and particularized short-term gains. The
latter include concessionary prices on parastatal output, preferential
access to credit, differential access to parastatal purchasing contracts,
and so on. Unlike the Argentine and more like the Chilean experience,
however, the sweeping reforms of Mexico's trade policy and its adoption of a more rational exchange rate policy have at least shut down
some of the traditional sources of rent seeking and begun to purge the
business sector of a number of the grosser allocational abuses of the
past.

A second metaphor has to do with external understanding of
Mexico's public sector decision making and the universal issue of transparency. Most students of Mexican policy have at times had the sensation
that they were pursuing a squid. Just as the subject swims into view, out
squirts the ink to add a protective ambiguity. So it is with privatization.
Not even in Argentina are accurate and exact data on privatization so hard
to come by. The information available on Mexican privatizations—save in
such major cases as the closure of Fundidora Monterrey or the sale of
major companies like the Presidente hotel chain and Mexicana de Cobre—
is both fragmentary and contradictory. Further, the Mexican process for
implementing privatization is dispersed over an ill-defined but apparently broad assortment of decision-making nodes, more dispersed than in
Argentina and much more so than in Brazil or Chile. Both the anatomy
and the configuration of the parastatal sector lacked definition to begin
with, before the privatization program was even suggested. Because of
this amorphous structure, very little about the past or future direction of
the program is or can be known outside the inner councils of state.[3] It
seems doubtful that the degree of imprecision in the conduct of the Mexican program is other than studied.

A marked contrast is offered by the other cases that compose this volume. Although in both the Dominican Republic and Trinidad and Tobago the interpenetration of private and public is no less pervasive than it is elsewhere—the non-Latin cultural heritage of the latter having produced little apparent difference in this regard—the relation is much less shrouded owing to the small and personal social systems in which the two sectors interact. Further, the economies of the two are, as William Demas, head of the Caribbean Development Bank, has put it, structurally open to a degree unmatched by any of the other countries, though whether their policies have always been compatible with this openness is another matter. This has meant that the more confined range of policy options available to public authorities in the two countries has left less policy space in which to maneuver. This, in turn, has given the whole process a clarity missing in the more complex environments of the larger countries. The Dominican Republic and, in lesser measure, the Trinidad and Tobago cases also show how deeply ingrained institutional patterns tend to bleed through the overlay of later social changes.

Strikingly different from the other cases is that of Brazil. Although its economic structure is more complex and its social and political structures no less intricately nuanced, and although the uncertainty in its political future is at least as great as that in any of the other instances, a remarkable continuity underlies the ebb and flow of policy events. Under President Jose Sarney, the country had seemingly lost its rudder, thanks to a distracted presidency and a legislative branch ensnared not only in politics-as-usual but also in applying its political habits to the writing of a constitution. Yet through it all the parastatal sector has exhibited a measure of autonomy that almost makes Brazil's political issues seem epiphenomenal. More than in Chile but less than in Argentina, Mexico, the Dominican Republic, and Trinidad and Tobago, the privatization program in Brazil is debt driven. Yet to a curious degree it appears rather less controversial than the privatization effort in any of the other national arenas, save Chile.

In Brazil a modest amount of reprivatization has already been competently carried out under the auspices of a lead institution, the Banco Nacional de Desenvolvimento Econômico e Social, BNDES, very much as the Corporación de Fomento de la Producción, CORFO, has ridden at the helm in Chile. More seems destined to take place in the years ahead. This is likely to be followed by at least some privatizations in the usual, formal sense of the term—the divestiture of enterprises that have always operated in the state sector. Indeed, a start has already been made with the disposition of the Caraíba copper refining company, though this did not occur without some friction from the private sector. On the other hand, MAFERSA (Material Ferroviaria, S.A.) has not yet been privatized despite protracted discussion of the desirability of doing so. At the same time, the confidence traditionally enjoyed by the Brazilian parastatal sector has permitted a versatile approach to privatization, including a great deal of both semiprivatization (that is, the joining of public capital and management and private capital and management in mixed enterprises) and simulated privatization (requiring that parastatal management emulate the performance norms of private enterprise). Neither variant is particularly new in the Brazilian context, and certainly not an innovation of the past few years. Brazilian parastatals—endowed in many cases, like those of Chile, with a relatively technocratic and professional management—long ago began to enter joint ventures with both domestic and foreign private capital. For that matter, a number of state-owned enterprises have more than held their own in competitive foreign markets, among them the Banco do Brasil (a far-flung commercial banking network); BRASPETRO (the overseas arm of the national oil company, PETROBRAS); the Companhia Vale do Rio Doce, or CVRD (a huge minerals conglomerate); and, perhaps above all, the Empresa Brasileira Aeronáutica, or EMBRAER (the government's aircraft manufacturer). It is true that the recent ups and downs of the Brazilian economy have throttled down the progress of privatization but less so, apparently, than in either Mexico or Argentina.

The Wider Context

Confronted with mounting budgetary costs for administration and social programs, for debt service, and for covering the parastatals' losses, governments everywhere have had to recognize that the traditional tools for ensuring high employment levels—expansionary fiscal and monetary policies, industrial protection, nationalization of bankrupt companies, and expanding the payrolls of state-owned enterprises—have run their course. The increasing interdependence of national economies, moreover, has prompted a greater awareness of the need to improve cost and product competitiveness in the internationally exposed sector. This, in turn, has implied attending to pent-up requirements of structural adjustment and removing supply impediments to faster growth in the private sector.

Other policies have, of course, figured prominently in recent discussion—for example, policies to bring down inflation and measures to raise savings. Encouraging the creation of more small firms—to enhance the employment effects of new investment and to improve income distribution—has also caught the attention of policy makers, not least because of the contemporary interest in the informal sector. Currently on the agenda, too, are policies to effect a regional deconcentration of economic activity, along with an exploration of ways to promote the generation and wider diffusion of, and adaptation to, new technologies.

To the degree that officials have relied on social pacts to convert at least some policy variables into constants, distributional issues have necessarily come back into the picture as well. Reactivating capital inflows through a more favorable climate for foreign investment has emerged as yet another policy objective, even in places that a few years ago beat the drums of suspicion whenever multinationals were mentioned. Through it all, the policy community in Latin America has developed a heightened awareness that today's level of interdependence has not only improved opportunity but also increased vulnerability, as in the greater volatility of exchange rates and the larger scale on which capital moves across borders—mostly on the way out. In their quest for a possibly chimerical degree of systemic stability, Latin American governments now find that policy management within countries is almost as complicated and difficult as the coordination of policies among countries, the shoal on which Latin American regional integration has foundered repeatedly.

The policy agenda of Latin American governments, then, is both cluttered and, despite the spread of a sort of developmental agnosticism, vigorously contested and beset by severe debt and balance-of-payments difficulties. Such circumstances are almost guaranteed to forestall resolute action by public authority, save in exceptional instances such as the bold liberalization decisions made by Chile in the 1970s and Mexico in the 1980s. In this context, it is no surprise that privatization has rarely held its own as an abiding concern to which policy makers are unshakably committed. On the contrary, it is nearly always perched, somewhat precariously, on the ledges of "larger" preoccupations, neglected even when it is not actively opposed. And opposed it often is, especially by the formidable "state bourgeoisie" that populates the machinery of government and the labyrinthine precincts of the myriad public enterprises, decentralized agencies, and autonomous organizations that make up the parastatal sector.

Several other factors reinforce the marginality of privatization in the policy debates that enliven Latin American capitals these days. One is that the past half-decade or so has dealt the Latin American business community a hard blow, giving it plenty to worry about in its struggle for survival and draining it of the funds that might be needed to take on and modernize operations now limping along under state management—those which from a social viewpoint are most in need of transfer to the private sector. Second, with the exception of firms like those to be mentioned shortly, relatively few economic undertakings in the government portfolio appeal to local investors, bedeviled with enough problems of their own without taking on others accumulated through years of desultory public management.

It is pertinent here to refer to two contrasting metaphors that have recently appeared in public discourse to describe the state's business dealings. Public officials, thinking of the many private firms governments have rescued from financial extinction, have inclined toward a hospital metaphor, one that portrays government as kindly physician. In this view, the numerous firms on the sick list are in various stages of recovery, so that reprivatization is simply a means of hastening their departure from the infirmary. Business commentators, however, are prone to use a kennel metaphor, doubting that the state as kennelmaster has been able to deflea the dogs to make them ready for return or sale to private owners. Between these opposing perceptions lies imperfectly charted territory, and the actual potential for privatization or reprivatization, contrasted with what will simply have to be closed down, is largely a matter for conjecture.

No doubt foreign capital could, in many cases, rectify the legacy of lengthy managerial ineptitude, whether public or private or a mixture of both. Nevertheless, not all the nationalistic sensibilities of the past sixty years or so have been laid to rest. Not by any means. The situation is accentuated by an overriding objective of sound management: the elimination of labor redundancy that pits foreign owners against local workers and middle-level managers and other professionals. Thus, political leadership has been understandably reluctant to open old wounds by peddling its assets on any great scale to foreigners. This, perhaps as much as fear of inflation, has inhibited a large-scale disposition of parastatals through debt-equity swaps. From the other side of the market, however, only the prospect of unusually favorable terms for recovering some value from past lending will, in most instances, induce foreign capital into reprivatization and privatization programs, given competing new investment opportunities elsewhere on the global horizon.

Looked at closely, then, privatization loses some of the appeal that surrounds it in more abstract and sometimes evangelistic discussions of its possibilities, particularly in the United States and the United Kingdom. Context makes all the difference. Further, differences in setting run even more deeply than the foregoing remarks suggest. It is not simply that buoyant capital markets facilitate the removal of public sector assets to market-tested management in the industrially advanced countries, and that the damaged and still immature capital markets of Latin

America are not up to the job. It is also very much to the point to question what can be assumed about local private sector management. Many firms have, after all, fallen into the hands of government lending institutions through receivership, having been unsuccessfully operated by their erstwhile private owners. What is more, whereas the caliber of governmental management may be gauged by the level of operating deficits, that of private management must often be judged against the levels of effective protection built into trade policy and enhanced by oligopolistic structure. Both of these have historically allowed many Latin American businesses to hold competition at arm's length. Private enterprise, in other words, is not everywhere synonymous with efficiency.

Nor is public enterprise necessarily synonymous with maladroit management. The point bears repeating, given the widespread assumption, in Latin America and abroad, to the contrary. Brazil's PETROBRAS, for example, has been commendably free of the problems that have plagued Mexico's PEMEX and Argentina's YPF. The Venezuelan government's oil companies have likewise displayed high-quality executive leadership, as have Venezuela's forays into the aluminum industry. EMBRAER is making its way quite successfully into international markets that make no concessions to inexperience and leave little or no room for lackadaisical business methods. Mexico's Nacional Financiera (NAFINSA), like Chile's CORFO, has garnered professional respect for the quality of its operations, while Corporación Nacional del Cobre de Chile (CODELCO–Chile), the large Chilean parastatal in the copper field, has earned high marks for managerial capability in a country that harbors, at the official level, no sentimental feeling whatever for the asserted advantages of state ownership.

To be useful as a guide for policy, therefore, privatization must be put into context. For Latin America, this means giving it a definition that seems broad but that actually pins it firmly to the social efficiency target assumed in discussions in the United States and Western Europe. Decisions made at the enterprise level must be disciplined by competitive market forces. In a business environment with a tradition of rent-seeking behavior, the removal of public assets to private ownership brings no automatic guarantee of improved performance and innovativeness. Transfers may even add to the concentration of property and disparities in income distribution. On occasion, therefore, improved public management may represent a surer form of "privatization." In other instances the market might dictate outright liquidation. This extended understanding of privatization serves as the operating assumption on which most of the following chapters are based. Simulated privatization, semiprivatization, liquidation, and peripheral privatization (the contracting out of segments of public operations) are all plausible alternatives to the formal privatization that usually figures as the centerpiece of discussion.

One final point needs to be made explicit to place privatization against other policies in Latin America. The attempted disengagement of government from much of its direct intervention in the economy does not ordinarily imply a "retreat of the state" in any aggregate sense, as statists have alleged and antistatists have hoped. Much remains to be done, in most countries, to get the fiscal house in order. Yet so vast are the unmet needs for public investment in social overhead projects and infrastructure, and for government spending on elemental welfare, that it is hard to imagine a future in which public sector activity would actually contract. It is a question, rather, of realigning priorities and diverting funds now absorbed in underwriting inefficiency to uses that benefit the needier segments of society and build the human and organizational capital on which broad economic advancement in the late twentieth century and beyond necessarily rests. Mexico's President Carlos Salinas de Gortari made this social case for privatization pointedly in his October 1989 State of the Union address:

> It is not a question of discussing whether the private sector is a better administrator than the public sector, or who is better at doing business. There are honorable and very competent public administrators. But the focal point of the state reform is to reach decisions that benefit the people, to resolve the dilemma between property to be managed or justice to be dispensed, between a more proprietary state or a more just state.

Privatization in Chile

PART 1
The Path to Privatization in Chile
José Piñera

The free-market economic revolution that took place in Chile after 1973 was the most radical departure from socialism that occurred anywhere in the world during this period. Even Prime Minister Margaret Thatcher's turnaround pales in comparison to the Chilean case, both because the extent of state interventionism in the Chilean economy had been deeper than in Britain and because the dash toward market forces in Chile encompassed not only the productive sectors but also critical areas in the social sector, such as social security, health, and education.

When discussing the privatization experience in Chile, it is important to bear in mind that it was part of a larger process of structural change designed to transform Chile into a free-market economy.

The Privatization Process

State entrepreneurship has a long tradition in the Chilean economy. Channeled mainly through the Corporación de Fomento de la Producción

(CORFO), a state-owned holding corporation and development bank created in 1938, public companies and corporations were managed by the state as economic policy tools. They were viewed not only as productive firms but also as mechanisms for altering income distribution and achieving other nonentrepreneurial goals. These government enterprises were overstaffed, bureaucratic, politicized, and inefficient. By the end of Eduardo Frei's administration in 1970, the state assumed sole or majority ownership of forty-four companies, held between 10 and 50 percent of the shares in two others, and had less than 10 percent of the stock in another four.

The companies of the parastatal sector were the largest and most important industrial operations of the country. They included, among others, the Empresa Nacional de Electricidad (ENDESA), the Compañía de Acero del Pacífico (CAP), and the Empresa Nacional de Petróleo (ENAP).

After the dramatic political changes at the end of the Frei period, state ownership of corporations peaked under the ensuing government of President Salvador Allende (1970–1973). More than five hundred companies came into government hands during those years, including nineteen commercial banks. The government acquired firms through several mechanisms, including an aggressive use of CORFO's investment function, loopholes in Chilean laws, and outright seizure, with or without the pretext of a labor conflict. Many of the transfers during this period were illegal. Once in the parastatal sector, the nationalized companies were used for absorbing existing unemployment, for promoting the government's policy, or for other political purposes.

With the concurrent rapid expansion of many agencies in the established administrative structure of the state, the ballooning of the parastatal sector far surpassed the government's managerial capacity. Administrative chaos was widespread, not only in the newly established and newly acquired parastatals but in the older parastatals as well. The deterioration was so severe that many state enterprises were unable to prepare their annual financial reports, and by all accounts the new "management" was frequently divided internally along ideological lines. Hence, conflicting preferences joined general ineptitude as an obstacle to the orderly conduct of business and industrial operations. By the end of 1973, the parastatal companies showed losses of more than US$500 million. Most of this was financed through a monetary expansion that resulted in huge inflation. The rise in prices reached 1,000 percent during the last year of the Allende government.

An equally dramatic shift in economic policy occurred in 1973, as a consequence of the change of government. The goal at the time was to lay the foundations of a free-market economy characterized by deregulation and liberalization of most markets; opening of the economy to foreign competition and foreign investment; social reforms affecting pensions, trade unions, health care, education, and training; and macroeconomic equilibrium. Privatization was seen as an integral part of this policy package in terms of enforcing market discipline at the microeconomic level and thereby making better use of resources and prodding firms to become more innovative.

Since the economic turnaround in 1973, Chile's privatization program has undergone three distinct phases:

1974–1981. Most of the private companies and corporations that came under government control during the Allende administration (approximately 250–350) were returned to their original owners in a massive reprivatization program. CORFO also sold its interest in 156 companies that had been acquired during the Allende administration and liquidated another 47, selling their assets. Some of the subsidiaries owned by CORFO companies were also divested, as were a considerable number of real properties, both urban and rural. Simultaneously, CORFO set about reorganizing its own structure and operations. This streamlining helped restore CORFO's ability to manage the large parastatals that remained in its charge. At the same time, CORFO took steps to put the managerial house in order in the remaining large parastatals, whose administration had suffered during the Allende period.

This privatization effort yielded revenues of around US$1 billion. Eighty percent of these revenues were realized between 1974 and 1979. The companies involved had been so mismanaged before privatization that many were able to increase production with only a fraction of their previous staffs.

In 1980, the privatization of Chile's pension system was approved. The privatization plan carried major implications for strengthening the capital market and moving toward pension-fund capitalism. The privatization of the pension system and other subsequent changes set the stage for a considerable expansion of employee stock ownership plans in the country. In time, these changes allowed the privately run pension funds to place their funds in privatized firms, including electricity companies, the local-service telephone company, the long-distance telephone company, the nitrate company, and a pharmaceuticals firm, among others. Besides authorizing pension funds to include these blue-chip investments in their portfolios, the changes included some precautionary restrictions: for example, the pension funds could place only a limited amount of resources into a company in which there was a dominant shareholder, and they were also limited in the amount they could hold in any single company.

1982–1984. Chile's 1982–1984 recession provoked a widespread financial crisis and led to a partial reversal of the earlier privatization effort.
Many of the domestic conglomerates that purchased the companies privatized during the 1974–1979 period operated with a high degree of
leverage.

In 1982, however, international lending to Latin America dried up
because of the Mexican debt crisis, and Chile was hit by a recession.
Moreover, in the wake of misguided internal macroeconomic policy in
Chile—essentially trying to maintain a fixed exchange rate for too
long—local interest rates reached unprecedented real levels. As the
exchange rate collapsed, the local currency equivalent to foreign obliga-
tions rose. This development impaired the solvency of the conglomerates' companies, as well as that of their associated banks. The
government intervened in the banks, along with the domestic
conglomerates' parent holding corporations, bringing more than fifty
enterprises and banks back under direct government control.

1985–1989. Between 1985 and 1986, the government introduced a program to reprivatize companies brought down by the crisis, distributing
their property to a broad range of owners and recapitalizing these enterprises. This new program was another important step in the broader
dissemination of economic information and the strengthening of the
capital market. By this time there was also stronger appreciation of the
need to distribute property more broadly, in order to stabilize the political system.

At first, the 1985–1988 privatization effort, in which approximately
fifty thousand investors participated, took three different forms: (1) small
package sales of stocks to a large number of investors (Banco de Santiago
and Banco de Chile); (2) large package sales to solvent domestic or foreign
investors (Copec, Inforsa, CCU); and (3) a mixture of both (the Provida
and Santa María pension funds). Between 1987 and 1989 a fourth feature
was added: the privatization of major government-owned companies that
had never been privately held.

The small package sales were called *capitalismo popular*. Small investors were offered advantageous terms to encourage their participation. These favorable terms—which amounted, in fact, to subsidies for
the *capitalistas populares*—included fifteen years of interest-free loans on
95 percent of the investment (with a 30 percent discount if payments
were made on time) and tax breaks. The subsidies were justified on the
basis that widespread ownership was good in itself, though they obviously violated the strict canons of free-market economies.

These years also witnessed the privatization of several of the large
public corporations still in government hands, mainly public utilities

and mining companies. It is in this area that Chile has moved farthest beyond the privatization programs of other Latin American countries.

It is important to note that at the beginning of the 1980s Chile's public corporation law was reformed to allow better protection for minority shareholders. Since then, all the privatized corporations have been obligated to distribute at least 30 percent of their profits. They have also been subject to much more rigorous requirements in the disclosure of financial and other information needed for improving investor decisions, an important change for the capital market as a whole.

Not surprisingly, new regulatory regimes were needed to define the price structure for services of the privately owned public utilities inasmuch as they are natural monopolies. For example, electricity is priced according to its marginal cost, and oil according to its import parity. The pricing rules are determined by state laws, making their modification difficult.

Privatizing the Pension System

In November 1980 the law that privatized the Chilean pension system was enacted (D.L. 3500). The new system went into effect on May 1, 1981, as a truly unique feature of Chilean privatization. Chile's traditional, government-operated "pay-as-you-go" social security system had been unfair and complex. With over one hundred different programs, depending on the type of worker, administration was inefficient and unwieldy. The system contained built-in incentives to underdeclare earnings in early years and overdeclare in later years since the pension a worker ultimately received depended on the last years' declarations. Moreover, it favored workers who had more access to the political system. General discontent with the system's inability to pay out pensions that fairly reflected an individual's contribution eventually resulted in pension reform.

The new social security system is an improvement in all respects. Not only does it promise better old age and survivors' pensions, but it has also contributed to the creation of a fairly efficient and advanced capital market, with an accompanying improvement in the productivity of resource allocation. Currently, the pension system consists of twelve privately managed pension funds (Administradoras de Fondos de Pensiones, or AFPs). New pension funds can be formed if the administration complies with a minimum capital requirement and other standard regulations decreed by the Superintendency of AFP, a government agency. Both foreign and nationally owned pension-management companies have been set up. These AFPs apply the workers' contributions (a minimum of 10 percent of their gross income, tax free) to personal capitalization accounts. For their part, the workers can choose the AFP they prefer and can change from one to another freely.

The government guarantees a minimum pension if an individual's accumulated funds are insufficient to provide a predefined minimum income by retirement age (age sixty-five for men, age sixty for women). After nine years of operations, the pension funds now manage approximately US$6 billion, equivalent to about 25 percent of gross domestic product (GDP). By the year 2000 these funds will likely represent approximately two-thirds of GDP. The Superintendency of AFP determines the different financial instruments in which the funds can be invested. It also determines maximum limits by instrument, issuer, and conglomerate. For the moment, the funds cannot be invested abroad. Investments in shares were allowed only after 1985, when the second great wave of privatization began.

All of the pension funds are channeled through the domestic capital market, where a maximum of 50 percent can be invested in government instruments. Within the limits already noted, money can also be put into shares of companies. The national savings accumulated in the pension funds is a high percentage of private financial savings.

These privately managed pension funds have been crucial to the success of the recent privatization process; the AFPs were one of the major buyers of shares of the firms privatized in this phase. Not coincidentally, they also constitute a guarantee of the whole process, since reversing past steps toward privatization would now affect the pensions of over 3 million Chileans.

ENERSIS: A Case Study

A case study of the privatization of an important company should illustrate how the process has evolved. At the end of 1987, the author was nominated chairman of the board of ENERSIS (formerly CHILECTRA Metropolitana), to represent the workers-shareholders.

ENERSIS distributes electricity to 1 million clients in Chile's capital city. Created in 1921 with private funds, it was nationalized in 1970, and fully privatized in the period 1983–1987. Table 2.1 shows the evolution of the privatization process of this firm by share of ownership.

The privatization of ENERSIS started slowly with issuance of shares to new clients as a means of covering the costs of needed equipment. Its employees, who own about 28 percent of the company, bought stocks in four phases:

TABLE 2.1	ENERSIS Ownership, 1982–1987 (percentage)					
Owners	1982	1983	1984	1985	1986	1987
State	100.00	98.96	95.85	83.67	38.06	0.00
Private	0.00	1.04	4.15	16.33	61.94	100.00
SOURCE: Author.						

- November 1985—The employees were offered the option of using up to 50 percent of their severance payments to buy stocks, sold at the average price observed in the stock market. During this phase, 71.3 percent participated, purchasing 7.8 percent of the company.

- October 1986—By this date, employees could use an additional 20 percent of severance payments to purchase stocks; 98 percent of the employees together purchased 3.15 percent of the company.

- June 1987—An additional 20 percent of severance payments was made available for stock purchases, and 96.4 percent of employees bought 3 percent of the company.

- July 1987—Creating two highly leveraged (10-to-1) companies specifically for this transaction, ENERSIS employees purchased 21.6 percent of the company.

In October 1986, 6.5 percent of company stock was sold in the stock market. In July 1987, an additional 12 percent was sold in the stock market, of which Security Pacific Bank bought 9.9 percent through the debt-equity swap program. The remaining shares were sold to small investors through the stock market and to the pension funds. The company's ownership structure at the beginning of 1990 was the following: employees, 26.9 percent; Security Pacific Bank, 9.9 percent; pension funds, 28.9 percent; and small shareholders (8,386), 35.8 percent. ENERSIS's privatization process was completely open and conducted at market prices.

After privatization, work-force productivity went up sharply, and unitary costs consequently declined. Since electricity prices have been relatively constant in real terms, the increase in yearly profits from around US$20 million in 1987 to US$60 million in 1989 can be attributed to efficiency gains. At the same time, the company has increased its investment levels from US$9 million in 1984 to US$35 million in 1989.

One example of better resource allocation within the company after privatization is the creation of Synapsis, a software development subsidiary. ENERSIS had a large pool of competent engineers who specialized in software development. To meet their main objective—efficiently managing the information associated with distributing electricity to the company's 1 million clients—these engineers produced many computer programs, leading ENERSIS to create Synapsis. After a few months of operation, 49 percent of Synapsis was sold to Unisys, the large American computer firm. Synapsis is now exporting software to the United States and has created a subsidiary in Colombia, and its prospects are excellent.

A Final Word

It is interesting to note the process's qualitative effects. A recent survey revealed that 47 percent of the population favored totally privatizing the big enterprises, 11 percent supported partial privatization, and 35 percent opposed it. Employees and the labor unions have radically changed their attitude toward the management of the firms and constantly seek means to improve their firms' efficiency. As a labor union leader stated in 1989, "Never before in the history of Chile have the workers had the possibility, like now, of being owners and identifying with the destiny and fortune of the enterprises where we work. When property is public, because it is everyone's property, it belongs to nobody."[1]

The new firm managers are pursuing new investment and diversifying their enterprises, thereby helping the economy's aggregate performance. They are also seeking to increase operational efficiency and to restructure their firms, with an eye to how the results are judged by shareholders and evaluated by the barometer of the stock market. Foreign mutual funds have been set up specializing in Chilean stocks, testifying to the attractiveness of the Chilean investment environment.

By many standards, the current privatization effort in Chile has been the most successful project of its kind in Latin America to date. Through the free market's allocation of resources, privatization has created more jobs and opportunities, contributed to faster economic growth, raised wages, and reinforced a free-market economic philosophy. The privatization of public utilities or natural monopolies has been accomplished in an efficient manner since marginal pricing schemes have been instituted for these firms. Beyond these gains, there is a social benefit in the wider distribution of property and in the consolidation of the newly privatized pension system.

PART 2
Further Observations on Chile
William Glade

The privatization effort in Chile is clearly the most significant such undertaking in Latin America and, as such, merits extended comment to round out the picture. Of the twenty-nine enterprises originally included in Chile's 1985–1988 privatization program, eight have been totally and twelve partially privatized, with the remainder now moving toward privatization. Property ownership has thereby been greatly diversified; the number of individuals owning stock has grown by 77 percent in the 1985–1988 period, from 26,604 to 47,167.

Although most of Chile's remaining parastatals are profitable, a moderate continuation of the privatization program should nevertheless bring a net social gain stemming from improved access to capital and foreign research and development. Privatization may have introduced more dynamic management and increased motivation among employees who now work in "their own" firms. The government has also benefited, not only from the receipt of considerable sums of cash but also from the higher taxes privatized firms will likely pay in the future.

The positive experience with debt-equity swaps should further improve the prospects for liquidating more of the external debt. Beyond these gains, there is a social benefit in the wider distribution of property and incentives for small investors, a noteworthy improvement in the financial position of pension funds, and the generally optimistic expectations for continued growth of the economy, with rising participation in the global economy and all the benefits that confers. While economic considerations have been paramount, the government has also sought, through privatization (and the reprivatization of assets confiscated in the early 1970s), to restore the legitimacy of private property.

That the process has run as smoothly as it has, embracing the traditional, old-line parastatals as well as the newer extensions of direct intervention, can be chalked up partly to the willingness of government to learn from its mistakes. But it is also partly attributable—and this cannot be overlooked—to the character of the state-owned enterprises that had been set up through the administration of President Eduardo Frei. Most of the pre-1970 parastatals were reasonably well managed. The problems the Chilean economy faced during the pre-Allende period came primarily from a low rate of capital formation and the intersectoral misallocation of resources (underinvestment in an agricultural sector that suffered from discriminatory policies), along with excessive protectionism for the manufacturing sector. Chronic inflation was also a problem, as it had been for decades, but it had not reached the levels that were to come in the 1970s.

With this history, there was in the initial veering toward privatization, through the reprivatization of firms seized by Allende, an unavoidable short-term consideration: namely, the practical managerial necessity of restoring economic order and resuming production. Indeed, this pragmatic imperative recalled the adoption of the New Economic Policy in the Soviet Union when the revolutionary government sought to repair the economic breakdown occasioned by its earlier embrace of wartime communism. But the diverse sources of the pre-Allende economic underachievement meant also that policy reorganization would have to go well beyond the mere question of asset ownership and deal with such larger issues as the systemic role of prices and the nature of Chile's engagement with the international economy. It is germane to note that, in the post-Allende period, besides working to improve the operating efficiency of its already established subsidiaries, CORFO was even involved in setting up a few new parastatals, two of which were established with foreign capital participation. Within a remarkably short time, moreover, the old-line mainstays of the parastatal sector had for the most part recovered their customary good management and operating efficiency, and moved gradually back to a commercially viable pay-as-you-go basis.

At the same time, serious mistakes were made during the first phase of the privatization. Many of the privatized companies were purchased by highly leveraged domestic conglomerates whose ability to snap up assets was greatly enhanced by their privileged access to the local financial market and by the subsidy provided by overvalued Chilean currency for borrowing abroad. In effect, the conglomerates used their control of commercial banks to tap the lower real interest rates prevailing in overseas capital markets and crowd out other domestic investors. There, as in Weimar Germany, conditions favored those who had access to foreign capital, and there, as in the heyday of finance capitalism, speculation on borrowed funds and the pyramiding of debt concentrated ownership and erected unstable corporate conglomerates. The structure of these conglomerates was to prove exceedingly vulnerable to collapse when initial reverses provided the trigger.

It was during this first wave of privatization that charges arose about the process's lack of transparency. Partly because of the government's inexperience on the pioneering road it was taking, and partly because of sheer haste in restoring legitimacy, these first divestitures were not as transparent as later ones. The process, however, was never as opaque as it was in Argentina until 1989 or, still more so, in Mexico. Undoubtedly, however, it was the disconcerting spectacle provided by the corporate buccaneers of the late 1970s, together with the perennial and pervasive squabble over asset valuation (a problem in all countries), that accounted for much of the unhappiness with the transparency issue. In view of the direction the privatization program would later take, however, it is interesting to note that as early as 1974 the sale of at least one company, the Compañia Sud-Americana de Vapores, a steamship company, involved both selling about half of CORFO's 46 percent interest on the stock exchange and negotiating the sale of the rest to the workers of the enterprise.

Ironically, in view of the government's commitment to liberal trade and international comparative advantage, it was the failure of a sugar company (that is, a company in a long-protected industry) that signaled, in the early 1980s, the onset of rapid collapse. As firm after firm was brought back under the shelter of state control during the financial debacle that began in 1982, popular jibes began to refer to the "Pinochet road to socialism," and the renationalized firms were soon christened the *área rara*, or odd sector.

It is worth observing that as of 1986, CORFO and the government together still held control of nearly forty enterprises, not including the "odd sector," but the most recent phase of privatization includes plans to turn twenty-nine of them over to private ownership.

Privatization of State-Owned Companies

The decision to privatize the parastatal sector incorporated a variety of goals. First, it sought to increase the economic performance of the enterprises, thereby enhancing the country's future development. Second, the method chosen, as well as the privatization itself, was to reinforce the free-market economy concept in the country by allowing more persons access to its direct benefits. Third, the process aimed to depoliticize economic decisions and decrease the strength of monopoly unions in the state-owned companies.

Privatization options were several. Employees of an enterprise with adequate resources could purchase their entire company through a down payment and long-term subsidized CORFO loans. The Empresa Chilena de Computación e Informática (ECOM), an informatics company, and the Empresa Electricidad Limari (EMEL), an electrical distributor, are in this category. Meanwhile, public utilities and two mining companies were completely privatized through mixed channels—AFP, debt-equity conversion programs, workers' programs, and sales to individuals in the stock exchange. Companies in this category are ENERSIS, a distributor of electricity in Santiago; Compañía Chilena de Generación Eléctrica (CHILGENER) and Compañía Chilena de Electricidad del la Quinta Región (CHILQUINTA), electrical generators; Sociedad Química y Minera de Chile (SOQUIMICH), a nitrate producer; and Compañía de Acero del Pacífico (CAP), a steel company. The government currently plans to fully privatize Empresa Nacional de Electricidad (ENDESA), a power company that is the largest public utility in the country.

Not surprisingly, new regulatory schemes were needed to constrain pricing and investment policies and other decisions of the privately owned public utilities, inasmuch as they are natural monopolies. For example, electricity is priced according to its marginal cost, and oil according to its import parity. The pricing rules are determined by state laws, making their modification difficult, but no one would claim that public utility regulation in the United States or anywhere else has reached the ideal. Under the circumstances, there was no practical alternative once the assets were transferred to private ownership in a noncompetitive market. Thus, despite the government's overall commitment to deregulation, in this instance it actually had to devise and impose new regulatory frameworks.

Public utilities such as Compañía de Teléfonos de Chile (CTC), the Chilean telephone company, which have additional capital requirements, are in many cases being privatized by issuing new stocks. In this way these enterprises have finally obtained the capital necessary to expand their facilities and meet demand. By early 1989, for example, almost half of the CTC had been sold to an Australian company. Although there was criticism of the transaction, it centered less on the divestiture as such than on the purchaser, a business conglomerate that had neither broad managerial experience in telecommunications nor command of the most advanced technology in this field.

Before initiating the privatization of these enterprises, however, the government proposed improvements in their operating efficiency and commercial viability. When there were "political" managers on the staffs of the firms, these were often replaced by "technical" managers, who continued after privatization. These privatized civil servants proved adept at making their firms profitable and efficient. Although their success was not surprising given CORFO's track record for effective administration—save in the early 1970s—it undermined the general ideological case against state management that was held as an article of faith by some of the new government's adherents.

Even though state-recruited management often proved to be expert, transfer to the private sector still held two advantages. First, it enhanced access to capital for expansion, often unavailable under government fiscal restraints. Second, it ensured, over the long haul, better access to the continuing stream of technological improvements.

The main criterion for determining the percentage of the public enterprises to be privatized was how much the market could absorb without significantly affecting the sale price. It was—and is—common for the government to increase the percentage of the firms to be privatized as privatization targets are reached. An example is ENDESA, for which the target went first from 30 to 49 percent and then to 100 percent of its shares held by private investors. To be sure, not all public enterprises have been put up for sale, and there is a disposition to retain some permanently in the government's hands as "strategic" companies. Corporación Nacional del Cobre de Chile (CODELCO–Chile), the national copper company, is the chief example. These are the exceptions to prevailing practice. It is entirely possible that a government of different political complexion might have a more elastic notion of what constitutes a strategic industry.

The management and financing of privatization transfers have taken several routes. For example, twenty-nine enterprises were evaluated before the latest and most refined of the Chilean privatization efforts, implemented in 1985–1988. All were internally evaluated, and many were evaluated by outside consultants as well. All were sold in good financial shape, and in some cases debts were transferred to CORFO (ENDESA's, for example).

The following types of sale procedures have been employed:

- Direct sale to new owners (foreign or domestic) according to highest bid. Examples include Empresa Hidroeléctrica Pilmaiquén, S.A. (purchased by Bankers Trust through debt-equity swap); Telex-Chile; Empresa Hidroeléctrica Pullinque, S.A.; Empresa Eléctrica de Atacama (EMELAT); Empresa Eléctrica de Coquimbo (EMEC); and Empresa Nacional de Explosivos (ENAEX). This procedure has been used mainly for relatively small firms.

- Partial sale to employees. A factor in practically all cases since 1985, this type of transaction generally offered better conditions to employees than to the other buyers. The goal was to sell at least 12.5 percent to the employees, thus enabling them to elect at least one employee to a board of seven directors. As of mid-1988, some fourteen thousand employees had participated.

- Sale of shares on the stock exchange, aimed at both small and large investors. These transactions, by and large, occurred through ordinary investment banking and stock brokerage firms.

- Popular capitalism. Aimed at the small investor, this procedure offered special deferred-payment programs with subsidized loans. Not all small-package offerings have been

equally generous, but all involved significant special inducements that may merit scrutiny by other countries seeking to
broaden their capital markets. Examples of this option are
the banks and the power company ENDESA.

- Partial sales to foreign investors. Examples of these are found
in CTC (the telephone company purchased by Bond Corporation) and SOQUIMICH (the nitrate producer purchased by
Kowa of Japan, Bankers Trust, and American Express). Debt-
equity swaps were used in the latter case but not in CTC.
Although the CTC case has been widely faulted for lacking
transparency and for the purchaser's lack of a track record in
telecommunications technology, the same concerns have not
been raised about most of the other transactions involving
foreign investment. Of all the firms in the wave of privatizations in the 1980s, only the CAP steel company case has attracted as much or even more criticism, but the CAP sale
involved domestic investors rather than foreigners.

- Sales to pension funds. These sales set prices at market value
or economic value in all cases. Generally only very small
percentages—and sometimes none—of these firms' shares
were traded on the stock exchange, making exchange quo-
tations a poor indicator of value. Economic values were
inferred through an evaluation procedure. Some special conditions or restrictions on ownership were imposed: No investor, except the government, could own more than 20
percent. Over 50 percent of the shares were to be divided
among shareholders who owned less than 10 percent individually. And at least 15 percent of the shares should be distributed among a minimum of 100 shareholders.

Post-Privatization Experience

Chile's privatization program is still in progress, and it is therefore too
soon to assess its quantitative effects. Nevertheless, one can observe
significant improvements in the average productivity of labor since the
change in administration of these enterprises.

Manufacturing exports grew by 35 percent in 1988, the best year on
record for Chilean exports in general. In the same year, foreign investment also set a record. The fall in unemployment has been dramatic. By
no means can all of this be chalked up to privatization, but it is relevant

that in 1988 several privatized companies—CTC, CAP, ENDESA, Empresa Nacional de Telecomunicaciones (ENTEL), SOQUIMICH, Compañía Chilena Tabacos (CCT), and CHILECTRA—were among the most profitable firms in the country. The profitability of other former parastatal firms—such as Gas Santiago, the airline LanChile, and a sugar producer Industria Azucarera Nacional (IANSA)—was reflected in substantial increases in the price of their stock. Meanwhile the fact that the government could still move ahead and propose the partial privatization of LanChile, the principal air carrier, and step up the sale of shares in companies already opened to private investors, indicates an expectation that the offers would be well received.

Obstacles to Implementing Privatization

Chile historically has had a very thin capital market, with relatively few potential buyers for the great number of enterprises to be privatized. This obstacle was approached by encouraging small investors through popular capitalism and advertising. The crucial element was incorporating the pension funds as buyers and allowing debt-for-shares schemes. In a few cases other techniques were used, such as allowing workers to capitalize their severance pay reserves, hitherto held by the corporations, by investing them in shares of the firms employing them.

The political factions that opposed the government also opposed this privatization process, claiming that the government was giving away state assets. The government responded by selling stocks to the workers through *capitalismo popular*. A good many privatization transactions were routed, in whole or in part, through the stock market, where a great deal of information is publicly available and where stock sales provide a market-based evaluation of assets and share prices. Using established investment banking houses, underwriting stockbrokers, and specialized consultants—to say nothing of competitive bidding—helped increase transparency further, but even so, did not quiet stories about alleged conflicts of interest. For example, rumors circulated about insider trading and government advisers ending up as shareholders in firms recommended for privatization. The truth of these charges, particularly in the privatizations carried out since 1985, is hard to ascertain. They may well not represent substantial infractions so much as occasional problems, but the possibility that some irregularities occurred now and then cannot be rejected out of hand, especially in light of recent highly publicized capital market scandals in New York and the recent insider trading problems in France, which implicated financiers close to government.

A further criticism related to transparency is that nontransparent transactions often allow little time for the independent study and authentication of data in privatization projects. The frequent use of qualified financial intermediaries and specialists in handling these transfers, especially since 1985, suggests that this criticism is much less valid today than in the early days of privatization. There has been a great deal of learning-by-doing in implementing the program.

Other criticisms range from allegations of favoritism in the selective preprivatization assumption of parastatal debts by CORFO, to criticisms that too few bidders have been involved in some transactions where "big-package" blocks of shares were offered. As in so many other cases, however—even that of CAP, the national steel company—the facts are not yet established, so there is ample room for both passionate controversy and dispassionate inquiry. Given the corrective actions taken after the earlier privatizations failed, though, there is little reason to believe that Chilean privatization since 1985 has been as plagued by these problems as other newly privatizing third world countries.

The Political Economy of Privatization in Mexico

Since 1982, the Mexican government has faced severe economic instability. In an attempt to ameliorate the situation during his term in office (1982–1988), President Miguel de la Madrid embarked on a series of economic reforms. These included liberalizing (opening up) the external sector and reducing the number of parastatal enterprises. The latter policy, informally called streamlining, is officially referred to as disincorporation. Both policies have been continued by the administration of Carlos Salinas de Gortari, who, as de la Madrid's secretary of budget and planning, was instrumental in the design and implementation of these economic policies.

This chapter analyzes and evaluates the extent and impact of the disincorporation of the Mexican economy. The first section examines the government's role in Mexico's economic development and in the growth of the country's public enterprises from the 1940s until 1982. During this time, public enterprises underwent three stages of development: a postrevolutionary economic revival, industrialization, and import substitution, which included buying out private sector companies in financial trouble. The second section provides a detailed description of the streamlining process of 1983–1988 and reviews the data available from various official sources. The final section interprets the administration's policy from both an economic and a political perspective. Because Mexico's disincorporation process is continuing, our conclusions are provisional, and more definitive conclusions must come later.

For reasons beyond the scope of this paper, until fairly recently the government held that the process of disincorporation was *not* privatization. Government development plans and other official documents referred to the disincorporation process as the process by which entities that were formerly part of the federal government lose the status of official public organizations or enterprises.

The entities subject to the disincorporation process may be commissions (usually advisory committees), trust funds (operative, financial, or both), or decentralized organizations (public producers of goods and services that are autonomous and whose budget and finances are supervised by Congress). Also, the government has sold its interests (share packages) in many private corporations—most of them listed on Mexico's stock exchange—which for a number of reasons it had acquired through time.

Disincorporation can take many forms: the sale of companies to the private or "social" sectors (such as unions and cooperatives); the transfer of entities to state or local governments; liquidation of public entities; and mergers between two or more public entities. In Mexico's steel sector, for example, enterprises merged and remained under government ownership. Enterprises in other sectors that were transferred to state and local governments remain under government control, albeit at a different level.

The Government's Role in Mexico's Economy

Although most analyses trace the formal beginning of government intervention to the 1917 constitution, it has been prevalent since the colonial era. As early as 1525, the Spanish Crown promulgated ordinances to control or regulate commodity prices in New Spain, and after 1580 the Crown established public granaries that fixed maximum prices and regulated grain supplies.[1]

Other public organizations were created during the colonial period. These *estancos*, considered by some to be the forerunners of public enterprises, were production and marketing monopolies in specific economic activities such as tobacco, mercury, salt, copper, tin, and gunpowder. These state monopolies were sometimes granted to private individuals as a concession or franchise, although this was not the rule. The government's ultimate aims when intervening in the economy were to regulate activities that might financially affect the Crown and to stimulate those that contributed to its hegemonic power.[2]

After independence in 1821, the Mexican state strove to foster previously restricted economic activities. The government created state financing institutions that provided credit to industries in these sectors. Not until the final years of the nineteenth century, however, did the Mexican government create and begin operating industrial and service companies like those in the country's present-day energy sector.[3]

The state and economic development in modern Mexico. The Mexican Revolution and the 1917 constitution mark the beginning of growing government intervention in economic affairs. An array of public institutions and legal provisions furthered the scope of the state's economic role and reserved key "strategic" sectors to the state. Foreign capital was banned in some sectors, and the state assumed broad regulatory powers over private activities and property to protect the public interest.

The 1917 constitution's provisions for the creation and expansion of government goals supported a highly pragmatic one:[4] The development of state enterprises speaks less to a "historic vision" or "nationalist conscience"[5] than to the government's need to reconstruct its economy after a decade of armed struggle. The Banco de México, created in 1925, might be viewed as modern Mexico's first public entity, even though the bank worked with private capital at the outset and aimed to "resolve the chaos in which the country's rather primitive banking system was involved." Some studies indicate that Mexico's early public corporations were "short-term oriented, lacking definite objectives, unsystematic."[6]

The development of public enterprises in Mexico since 1917 is traditionally divided into three different phases, defined by government objectives or the role public corporations were to play in the country's import-substitution strategy.[7] Together, these phases cover the 1925–1982 period.

1925–1946. The public enterprises dating from these years were intended to promote the renewal of orderly economic activity after the Revolution. These institutions include the Banco de México, established in 1925; Banco de Crédito Agrícola, 1926; Banco Nacional Hipotecario, 1933; Nacional Financiera (NAFINSA), 1934; Comisión Federal de Electricidad (CFE), 1937; Compañía Exportadora Importadora de Maíz (CEIM), 1937; Altos Hornos de México (AHMSA), 1942; and Guanos y Fertilizantes de México, 1943.

1947–1955. The administration's main economic policy objective during this period was to support the continuing industrialization process.

TABLE 3.1   Public Expenditure and Investment as a Percentage of GDP in Mexico
(annual average)

Years	Public expenditure/GDP	Public investment/GDP
1925–1934	6.74	2.50
1935–1954	8.88	4.88
1955–1969	15.88	5.90

SOURCE: NAFINSA, La economía Mexicana en cifras (Mexico City, 1984).

Public investments in energy, transportation, and widely used industrial inputs rose substantially to accelerate private capital formation.
Table 3.1 shows that public investment as a percentage of gross domestic product almost doubled from an average 2.50 percent between 1925
and 1934 to 4.88 percent between 1935 and 1954.

It was during this second phase that the federal government first
established mechanisms to control and coordinate public entities, not
only because of their growing economic importance, but also because
"there was a clear trend toward even greater future growth." This period witnessed the enactment of the first Law to Control Decentralized
Organizations and State Enterprises in 1947 and the establishment of
the National Investments Commission in 1948. The commission proved
ineffective, however, and was dissolved after one year. Its functions
were subsequently dispersed among various public agencies. Between
1949 and 1958, a number of other commissions were created and succes-
sive laws and regulations enacted—ostensibly to provide "flexible and
effective mechanisms for control and evaluation of state enterprises."[8]

1956–1982. This period's main characteristic was the government's resolve to participate directly in the import-substitution process, buying
out failing private sector companies and establishing enterprises in several branches of economic activity, including transportation equipment,
petrochemicals, and capital goods.[9] B. Rey Romay summarizes the
state's activities:

> Between 1940 and 1980, the state was founder of 111 industrial enter-
> prises; partner in another 124, in 35 of which it was "forced" to partic-
> ipate because of the companies' precarious situation, or because shares
> were received as repayment of credits that the original owners were
> unable to pay otherwise; and majority shareholder in 59 companies
> that were either state created or added to already existing holding
> companies.[10]

The proliferation of public companies led the federal government to
develop more global control systems. The first Law of Ministries and

State Departments was approved in 1958 to establish a coherent framework for the state enterprises' activities. Although legislative resolutions stressed the need to "control" government enterprises, their real objective was twofold: to adapt the legal framework to the evolutionary changes in public administration and to improve coordination between government revenue and spending programs, in which state-owned companies began to play an increasing role.[11] There was relatively little concern with the actual operations of the companies or with their economic or social justification.

The 1958 law was followed by two similar laws to control decentralized organizations and state enterprises, one passed in 1965 and the other in 1970. These laws set guidelines for public expenditure projects, approval systems, and the allocation of public contracts.[12]

A 1976 attempt to "reorganize" the general legal framework for the operation of state companies adopted a new approach: sectoral organization. To facilitate control of the companies and to avoid duplication and interference among federal agencies performing similar functions, each entity was assigned to a particular "sector" (or ministry), whose head was made responsible for its supervision. All of these legal and administrative efforts to improve coordination and control of state enterprises addressed the same problem: Growth in the number of federal entities was outstripping federal resources and mechanisms with which to plan and coordinate their operations.

Public Enterprise Growth

1940–1982. The growth of public enterprises is one of the most-discussed aspects of the Mexican economy. Stimulating the debate is the scarce and often contradictory information about the actual number and nature of public entities in existence. Analysts also differ over whether there are too many or too few government entities, depending on his or her political orientation.

For example, one faction holds that public enterprises arose in Mexico in response to a clear "historical vision or conscience" on the part of the Mexican state.[13] Proponents of this view assert that the number of enterprises is not excessive and that their creation was always justified, because they defended the public interest. Another common view holds that new government entities were created solely to fill "gaps" in the country's economic structure and to secure continued growth when private investors lacked the will or resources to develop specific sectors or activities, or when strategic sectors (such as oil and electric power) were controlled by foreign investors.[14] Finally, there are those who

TABLE 3.2   Number of Public Entities Registered in the Public Administration in Mexico, 1972–1982

	Decentral- ized organisms		Majority- owned enterprises		Minority– participation enterprises		Subtotal		Trust funds		Total		Differ- ence
	I	II	I	II	I	II	I	II	I	II	I	II	I – II
1972	n.a.	102	n.a.	169	n.a.	23	n.a.	294	n.a.	n.a.	n.a.	n.a.	n.a.
1977	129	145	500	422	59	54	688	621	210	197	898	818	80
1978	127	117	509	420	63	51	699	588	192	201	891	789	103
1979	131	110	510	420	61	53	702	583	196	178	898	761	137
1980	127	77	518	450	63	54	708	581	195	199	903	780	123
1981	88	78	520	505	63	51	671	634	201	206	872	840	33
1982	90	78	662	535	52	48	804	661	176	188	980	849	131

n.a. = not available.
SOURCES: I. Secretaría de Programación y Presupuesto, "Coordinación general de la administración pública federal," *Empresa pública: problemas y desarrollo* 1, no. 1 (1986).
II. Centro de Estudios Económicos del Sector Privado, A.C., "Las empresas estatales, la burocracia y la modernización" (Mexico City, 1986, mimeo).

assert that most state enterprises have displaced or crowded out private investors and brought the state into areas where its presence is unjustified and unproductive. Holders of this view point to the inefficiency, corruption, and huge deficits in public enterprises as the unavoidable consequences of government interference.[15]

Most of the literature on Mexico's public enterprises agrees that, until the 1950s, government participation in the economy was concentrated in a few sectors. Ramírez and Carrillo and García note that in the early 1950s there were only twelve public entities (excluding several development banks), most in transportation, oil, electricity, and fertilizers. This figure is contested by other studies however. Jesús González S. affirms that 151 entities existed in 1950, although he does not disclose his sources. Contradictions also arise regarding 1960 figures. Ramírez and Carrillo and García refer to only 29 public entities at this time, while González S. identifies 262. The larger number seems more realistic than the lower one, but there are no official data to support one figure or the other.[16]

More detailed information did not become available until the early 1970s, and it still contained inconsistencies. Table 3.2 indicates a sharp increase (from 294 to 621) in the total number of public enterprises between 1972 and 1977. The upward trend continued after 1977, albeit more slowly, mainly because the number of trust funds (*fideicomisos*) varied widely from year to year. The decrease in decentralized entities between 1977 and 1982 resulted primarily from the "sectorization" process, begun in 1977, through which many official entities were

TABLE 3.3   Total Public Sector and Public Enterprises' Share in Mexico's GDP, Employment, and Capital Formation (percentage)

Year	GDP Total public sector	GDP Public enterprises	GDP excluding PEMEX Total public sector	GDP excluding PEMEX Public enterprises	Employment Total public sector	Employment Public enterprises	Gross capital formation Total public sector	Gross capital formation Public enterprises
1975	14.6	6.6	11.9	3.9	14.0	3.4	41.9	26.0
1976	15.2	6.5	13.0	4.3	15.1	3.6	38.9	24.6
1977	16.4	7.8	13.2	4.6	15.3	3.7	39.8	23.8
1978	16.2	7.7	13.0	4.5	15.8	3.7	45.1	28.6
1979	16.9	8.3	12.9	4.3	16.4	3.8	43.8	27.7
1980	19.1	10.5	11.5	3.9	17.0	3.9	45.0	26.7
1981	19.8	10.4	13.5	4.1	17.5	4.0	46.3	29.2
1982	23.3	14.0	13.3	4.0	18.7	4.4	46.7	30.0
1983	25.6	18.2	12.5	5.1	20.4	5.1	44.5	27.7
1984	24.4	17.0	12.7	5.4	21.0	5.2	39.4	24.2
1985	22.8	15.5	12.3	5.4	21.4	5.2	35.8	22.2
1986	20.4	13.3	12.9	5.8	22.2	5.2	35.1	20.0

SOURCE: Secretaría de Programación y Presupuesto, *Cuentas de producción del sector público* (Mexico City, 1984 and 1987).

reclassified in hopes of improving federal controls over them and curtailing their independence through ministerial supervision.

Table 3.3 presents the public enterprises' share in GDP, employment, and gross capital formation (that is, investment) in comparison with the total public sector. All three measures have been rising since 1975, reflecting the increasing importance of the public sector in the economy and of government enterprises within the public sector. Opinions vary about whether this participation is too extensive or too limited. Many authors, including government officials, believe that the public sector's share of GDP—between one-fourth and one-fifth—attests to the public sector's limited role in the economy and the predominant role of the private sector.[17]

These figures grossly understate the importance of the public sector in economic life however. Because of the way the GDP figures are calculated, public enterprises that sell at heavily subsidized prices might have a negative value added. One example is Compañía Nacional de Subsistencias Populares (CONASUPO) whose sales volume consistently ranks among the five largest public enterprises in Mexico. Yet CONASUPO does not appear in national accounts, and this agency decreases the weight of the public sector in the economy. The same is true of other government entities.

TABLE 3.4   Public Enterprise Share of Total Production in Selected Mexican Industries, 1965–1982 (percentage)

	1965	1970	1975	1980	1982
Sugar	17.5	34.8	40.0	57.6	65.8
Fish and seafood products	3.4	42.0	14.8	11.9	26.5
Oil refining and derivatives	100.0	100.0	100.0	100.0	100.0
Basic petrochemicals	100.0	100.0	100.0	100.0	100.0
Fertilizers	44.0	61.3	61.1	62.8	66.1
Iron and steel industry	41.2	36.2	38.4	44.3	67.8
Automobile industry	9.1	21.2	23.7	23.3	18.5
Transportation equipment	92.4	51.9	41.9	51.1	61.7

SOURCE: W. Peres, "La estructura de la industria estatal," *Economía Mexicana* 4 (1982), Centro de Investigación y Docencia Económica, A.C., Mexico City; J. Tamayo, "Las paraestatales en México," *Investigación económica* (October–December 1987).

Another reason why these figures are unreflective of the public sector's role is the fact that major government enterprises act as monopolies or quasi-monopolies in several branches of economic activity, including oil, basic petrochemicals, fertilizers, and electricity (see Table 3.4). Hence, private production is totally or almost totally dependent on public suppliers and their pricing policies. The private sector, which frequently benefits from the subsidized inputs secured from these enterprises, confronts sharp and unanticipated price increases when they are removed. Further, the private sector is affected whenever supply problems arise in the public sector, either for technical reasons or because of inefficiencies. The products of these public enterprises cannot be freely imported. These considerations suggest that the importance of government enterprises transcends the figures on GDP and employment and extends to a "qualitative" dimension.

Nineteen eighty-two was a dramatic year for the Mexican economy. After three consecutive years of strong economic growth founded on rising oil income and external financing, the economy collapsed. Inflation neared 100 percent. Real GDP decreased for the first time in decades. Total external debt soared to US$87.6 billion. Real wages fell by more than 12 percent. The peso was devalued 267 percent over the year, and the public sector's financial deficit reached an astonishing 18 percent of GDP (see Table 3.5).

Although this collapse, the result of a steady deterioration that began in mid-1981, was not totally unexpected, the Mexican economy was set adrift for one-and-a-half years while it seesawed between one

TABLE 3.5   Selected Macroeconomic Indicators for Mexico, 1977–1982

	1977	1978	1979	1980	1981	1982
Real GDP growth (%)	3.4	8.2	9.2	8.3	7.9	−0.2
Inflation rate (%)	20.7	16.2	20.0	29.8	28.7	98.8
Current account balance (US$ millions)	−1,596.4	−2,693.0	−4,870.5	−10,739.7	−16,052.0	−6,220.9
Exchange rate devaluation (%)	14.0	−0.1	0.3	2.0	12.7	267.8
Foreign exchange reserves (US$ millions)	1,482.0	2,020.2	2,951.4	3,997.4	5,021.0	761.2
External debt (US$ millions)	30,293.0	35,094.0	42,370.0	54,426.0	80,998.0	87,588.0
Public sector deficit/GDP (%)	5.0	5.1	5.5	5.8	15.2	17.9
Public enterprises' deficit/public sector deficit (%)	108.9	107.1	104.7	113.9	73.4	50.1

SOURCE: Banco de México and Secretaría de Hacienda, annual reports, various years.

economic policy and another. As the crisis progressed, it spilled over into the political and social arenas, leading to the nationalization of the private banking system and the establishment of complete foreign exchange controls in September 1982. These two government actions produced the worst conflict between the private and public sectors in over fifty years and fueled unprecedented capital flight.

Immediately after taking office in December 1982, the de la Madrid administration announced its economic restructuring program, Programa Inmediato de Reconstrucción Económica (PIRE). Along with this ten-point program to address the most critical aspects of the crisis, the new government presented a three-point strategy for "structural changes" in the economy. Most PIRE measures were designed to correct the public sector's financial disequilibrium. Neither the PIRE nor the structural change strategy, however, contemplated selling off or closing down government entities. Although both stressed the need to modernize them, to operate them efficiently and honestly, and to reduce their deficits, there was no sense of an overexpanded public sector or of a need to reduce the number of government enterprises. At most, these two programs recognized that subsidies to public enterprises had ballooned out of proportion and that many subsidies never reached their intended beneficiaries.

Two factors argued against selling or closing some state enterprises. First, the fiscal deficit's contribution to macroeconomic imbalances was seen as an "income problem"—the result of insufficient government revenue—rather than a "spending problem." Second, the role of public enterprise in the economy continued to be regarded as crucial to the mixed economy model and to state guidance of the economy, a doctrine enunciated with emphasis by the new de la Madrid administration. In fact, the administration enacted a constitutional amendment during its first month in office that made the government constitutionally responsible for directing the economy under the National Planning System.

1983–1984. Discrepancies among data from different official sources continue to appear in figures on the number of government entities in operation during the 1980s. In his 1987 State of the Union address, President de la Madrid noted that there were 1,155 government entities in December 1982.[18] On November 15, 1982, however, the *Diario Oficial* counted 849 entities. Another official source gives a figure of 980, and still another puts the total at 912.[19] In outlining the broad trends of the disincorporation process during 1983 and 1984, we will take as reference the 1,155 total, since it is the figure that has been used consistently by official sources during the de la Madrid administration (although some recent figures put this total at 1,214[20]).

There are also significant discrepancies as to the extent of the disincorporation process in 1983 and 1984, even from the same governmental source. Thus, according to de la Madrid's fifth State of the Union address in 1987, the number of public entities disincorporated during the period was 99, while in the sixth address (1988) the figure was corrected to 118 without explanation. Other data from the Ministry of Planning and Budget show a reduction of 74 entities, and some government officials put the number at 23 (see Table 3.6).[21]

There appear to be two reasons for these variations in the official figures: first, the lack of a systematic register by the federal government of both the absolute number of public entities and the disincorporation process itself; and second, the frequent inclusion of entities authorized to be disincorporated (or in the process of disincorporation) as actual disincorporations.

Nevertheless, these reductions were hardly spectacular for several reasons. First, because there was official recognition of the role of the fiscal disequilibrium in the economic crisis, one might have expected the government to reduce the number of public entities more quickly. Second, if the de la Madrid administration was indeed "probusiness" or "neoliberal" as some analysts labeled it, it could have been expected to immediately implement a strong disincorporation program to repair the damage caused to relations between the public and private sectors by the bank nationalization of September 1982. Third, and perhaps most

TABLE 3.6   Number of Public Entities in Mexico according to Three Sources, 1982–1988

	Source of information		
Year	I	II	III
1982	980	1,155	1,155
1983	952	1,082	1,058
1984	916	1,056	1,037
1985		993	932
1986		889	732
1987		851	612
1988			449

Blank cell = not applicable.
SOURCES: I. Secretaría de Programación y Presupuesto, *Coordinación general de modernización de la administración pública federal.*
II. De la Madrid, *Quinto informe de gobierno.*
III. De la Madrid, *Sexto informe de gobierno.*

important, in the past there had always been variations in the number of public entities from one year to the next. Some entities, set up with short-term objectives, disappeared after a year or two (for example, the trust fund to finance and manage the 1979 World University Games and several funds to finance film making). In other cases, reorganizations and mergers between enterprises and their subsidiaries affected the total number. Some were in liquidation, a process that often lasted several years.[22]

Whatever the number of disincorporations in 1983–1984, the reduction in public entities was of relatively little significance since the total number at the end of 1984 was larger than at any time between 1977 and 1981.[23] Moreover, the bulk of such disincorporations were commissions, trust funds, and the like, since only eight industrial-sector government enterprises were sold and ten eliminated or liquidated during the 1983–1984 period.[24] These sales and liquidations reduced public production and employment very little (see Table 3.7).

1985–1988. On February 7, 1985, the federal government announced an economic adjustment program to offset a reduction of around US$300 million in oil revenues. The program would support an anti-inflationary program that had been weakening for several months; official inflation forecasts of 35 percent fell far short of the 63 percent inflation registered by year's end. The program included

• a 100 billion peso reduction in public spending through the cancellation of nonpriority investment projects

TABLE 3.7   Disincorporated Enterprises' Share of Total Gross Production and Employment in the Mexican Government's Nonoil Industrial Sector, 1983–1984

	Number of enterprises	Gross production[a] (%)	Employment[a] (%)
Enterprises sold	5	4.8	2.9
Enterprises to be liquidated	6	1.0	1.0
Total	11	5.8	3.9

a. In 1981.
SOURCE: J. Machado, W. Peres, and O. Delgado (1985).

- a 150 billion peso reduction in current expenditure

- liquidation, sale, or transfer to local governments of twenty-three government entities

- stronger tax enforcement

- accelerated liberalization of the economy and a relaxation of import quotas

- an additional export promotion program[25]

Of the 236 entities to be disincorporated, 65 were to be sold, 55 liquidated, and 7 transferred to local governments. These figures somewhat overstate the program's dimensions since 13 entities were already in a process of liquidation or extinction, and the government was a minority owner of 13 others. In addition, of the 236 total, only 83 were in fact enterprises. The remainder comprised trust funds, advisory boards or commissions, and the like. Moreover, 31 of these 83 were not in operation (14 of them existed only on paper).[26]

Even though this was the most ambitious disincorporation process ever announced in Mexico, it amounted to a reduction of about 10 percent in state manufacturing production from 1981 levels and a drop from 8.9 to 7.9 percent in the government's share of total manufacturing output. This led some authors to conclude that the disincorporations "did not significantly change the size of the government's industrial sector, though it somewhat diminished its diversity."[27] Moreover, the reductions achieved did not reach the officially projected level. Only 63 entities were disincorporated in 1985, and the overall economic impact was less than initially anticipated.

TABLE 3.8	Mexico's Disincorporation Process, 1983–1987				
	1983	1984	1985	1986	1987
Total number of entities (beginning of each year)	1,155	1,082	1,056	993	889
Disincorporations concluded	83	37	78	116	40[a]
Disincorporations "under study"	86	6	31	70	168
New entities	10	11	15	12	2
Actual number of entities (at year's end)	1,082	1,056	993	889	851
Projected number of entities[b]	996	964	870	696	507

a. Includes 17 more disincorporations that were reported as concluded in December 1987, with the announcement of a new economic strategy (Economic Solidarity Pact).
b. By the government.
SOURCE: De la Madrid, *Quinto informe de gobierno.*

Throughout 1986–1987, a number of official communiqués listed the entities to be liquidated, transferred, or sold. Some entities included on these lists were supposed to have been sold between 1983 and 1985,[28] while others had not previously appeared as registered entities.[29] Again according to official figures, in 1986, 116 government entities were disincorporated, 70 were "under study," and 12 were created. In 1987 there were 23 disincorporations, 168 under study, and 2 new creations.

The confusing assortment of figures on the disincorporation process can be explained by a number of factors. First, there has never been a definitive and complete list of all government entities. Second, although all disincorporations have been announced, there has been no follow-up on how many were concluded. Third, some entities have been offered for sale or liquidated more than once. (Oerlikon Italiana, put up for sale in 1984, was still being offered at the beginning of 1990.) And fourth, the government has adopted the policy of registering many disincorporations in the year that they are first announced and not when they are actually concluded. Thus, a fairly recent report by the Ministry of Planning and Budget to Congress stated that there were 12 disincorporations pending from 1985, 28 from 1986, 14 from 1987, and 65 from 1988.[30] For these reasons it seems more accurate to analyze the *process* of disincorporation from the figures released each year than from the more recent ones where a "retrospective" view is given. Table 3.8 summarizes official data on the disincorporation process presented in the 1987 State of the Union address.

Clearly, between 1983 and 1987 the total number of public entities disincorporated was significant, although the number did not reach the government's own projections. There was a reduction of 304 entities, of which 80 were sold, 76 liquidated, 34 merged with other public entities, and 114 either liquidated or merged. There are no figures, however, for the economic effects of these disincorporations on employment, production, or asset value. We may assume, however, that they were considerably smaller than the absolute numbers may suggest, since most of the disincorporated entities were commissions and trust funds; and in the case of enterprises, the great majority were relatively small or had low operating levels. Perhaps the most important exception to this was Fundidora de Monterrey (an old steel mill) that was declared bankrupt and closed down in 1986.

If we also consider the 168 entities for which there was a declared intent to disincorporate by the end of 1987, we can conclude that the government had ostensibly decided to reduce the total number of entities from 1,155 in 1982 to 683, that is, by 41 percent.

In December 1982 the government was involved in 409 industrial sector enterprises (though in some it was a minority participant). From 1983 to 1987, 129 enterprises were disincorporated, leaving 280 still in operation—a reduction of 31.5 percent. During 1988 the process continued at a fast pace, both because of new entities slated for disincorporation and because of the conclusion of disincorporations initiated in previous years. In contrast to previous years, in 1988 some important companies were disincorporated, such as Aeroméxico (the national airline) and some mining concerns and sugar mills (though in some cases the government retained minority ownership).

In 1988, 157 additional entities were authorized for disincorporation, of which 92 were concluded and 65 remained pending.[31] Overall, the total number of entities diminished from 612 in 1987 to 449 in 1988;[32] 71 of the disincorporations concluded in 1988 had begun in previous years. Finally, according to preliminary data, as of September 1989 the number of public entities was 389, which represents a reduction of 60 from December 1988.[33]

To conclude, two comments should be made about all these figures. First, though impressive, the reduction in absolute numbers of public entities (from 1,155 in 1982 to 389 in September 1989) does not necessarily imply a similar reduction (66.3 percent) in the size of the public enterprise sector or in its economic impact, as many government officials often point out. The reason is simple: with the exception of a handful of enterprises, the great majority have had little macroeconomic impact. The main public entities (PEMEX, CFE, Fertimex, CONASUPO, FFCC, etc.) have remained apart from the process, and as previously mentioned, there is no information regarding their economic impact; moreover, there also are vague data as to the amount of revenue raised from the sales to the private and social sectors. Available data put the net value of sales between 1985 and November 1988 at 1.58 trillion pesos (in constant terms), while other information indicates an amount of 2.5 billion pesos by September 1989.[34] Only as a reference, the public sector's financial deficit in 1988 amounted to only 31 trillion pesos.

Second, it is interesting to note that according to official sources, by the end of 1988 there still were 54 disincorporations pending from previous years: 12 from 1985, 28 from 1986, and 14 from 1987; buyers could not be found for most of them, but the government had nevertheless decided to continue trying to sell them rather than closing them down altogether.[35]

The Political Economy of Privatization in Mexico

Given its long-standing participation in economic activity, why has the government now chosen to redefine its economic role? This change in one of the basic tenets of the economic and political establishment has broad political and ideological implications.

Why did the de la Madrid administration decide to adopt a program as controversial as disincorporation—a program bound to attract criticism both inside and outside government—as one of its main features? And once having decided to do so, why did it wait to announce its disincorporation program until its third year in office?

In his presidential campaign, de la Madrid stressed the need for efficiency and honesty in public enterprise management. He recognized that strong government did not necessarily mean big government. His concern with efficiency and integrity in public enterprises was not new. His words were reminiscent of a call to reorganize the public enterprise sector—even to close or sell enterprises that were not "wholly justified"—issued ten years earlier:

> The chaotic, short-term-oriented and unprogrammed growth of the public sector, particularly the decentralized sector [i.e., government enterprises], has led to important imbalances between those ministries that, in theory, should have acted responsibly to every sector.[36]

A few years later, the López Portillo administration (1976–1982) undertook an administrative reform "to prevent the public sector's irrational or excessive growth" and to ensure "greater efficiency, effectiveness, and coherence of the public sector's entities with national economic policy."[37]

Ironically, it was de la Madrid's administration that promoted a constitutional amendment to make explicit the government's responsibility for economic leadership. This administration also designated banking services as a strategic sector reserved to the state, thus thwarting any attempt to reverse the bank nationalization. The disincorporation process represents a move away from the concept of "government as entrepreneur." The reasons for this shift are extremely important in terms of the political economy of government behavior.

Does privatization mean redefining the public and private sectors' roles in the economy and liberalizing the economy in order to allow a freer role for "market forces," while the government concentrates on its "natural" responsibilities? Or does it reflect the state's recognition that it cannot effectively perform economic activities and that the private sector is more efficient—hence the transfer of public enterprises to this sector? If we accept the second definition, then there has been no privatization in Mexico.[38]

On the contrary, the constitution's "economic chapter" remains intact. It gives the government exclusive rights in many economic areas and protects its future entry into any sector it considers strategic or a priority. Moreover, most disincorporations were simply closures of entities like trust funds that were oriented toward specific projects, rather than sales of productive companies. The government continues to stress its ability to manage enterprises, many of which guarantee Mexico's sovereignty and economic independence, objectives that the private sector is supposedly unable to achieve because of its self-interest. The following section considers several alternative explanations or hypotheses—including the official one—for the government's decision to pursue the disincorporation process.

Alternative Explanations for Disincorporation

The official explanation. According to public statements and related documents (there being no formal document setting up the disincorporation program), the program aimed to "rationalize the size and operation of government enterprises, in order to achieve greater efficiency in pursuing objectives within strategic and priority sectors." The resources freed by disincorporation were to strengthen official participation in other areas.[39] From the official perspective, disincorporation is essentially an efficiency measure. Past government overexpansion in economic activities dictated the current reduction in scope in order to enhance efficiency.

Past administrations had announced programs to do the same but never carried them out.[40] Why, then, did the de la Madrid administration actually pursue this oft-promised policy? And why did it wait until 1985 to do so? If economic efficiency had been a constant preoccupation since de la Madrid's inaugural address, why did it take so long to implement the disincorporation program? One could say that both program details and public opinion had to be carefully "prepared" before announcing the program. However, the process's slow pace and intermittent internal contradictions suggest the opposite.[41]

A pragmatic explanation. A second possible explanation is that the government's near bankruptcy in 1982 forced it to sell or suspend entities. This inference has a major flaw, however. Although the public entities' deficit was indeed a determinant of total public deficit, particularly until 1980 (see Table 3.5), its relative contribution to this deficit diminished in 1981 and 1982. Officialdom refutes the government bankruptcy theory and points instead to a twofold cause of the public enterprise sector's precarious financial position: Prices on public enterprise output had deliberately been kept low as an anti-inflationary strategy, and oil income was expected to subsidize other sectors.[42] When oil revenues fell, public enterprises found themselves in economic difficulty.

Moreover, even though more extensive adjustments were made in the 1985–1987 period, the fiscal deficit remained large. Sixty-five percent of this deficit was attributable to the seven largest public enterprises (excluding PEMEX), and none of these was ever mentioned as a prospect for disincorporation. Thus, the savings that were made were insignificant in relation to the actual magnitude of the financial requirements of the public sector.

An ideological explanation. As noted above, de la Madrid did not announce his disincorporation program until well into his term. His early years had a much different emphasis, reflected in one of his first acts—enacting a constitutional amendment to support the state's governance of the economy. As proponents of this view argue, however, the persistence of the economic crisis after two years of economic austerity and public spending restraint might have led the administration to move toward the right, disincorporation being one result of this ideological shift.

Although this hypothesis cannot be easily confirmed or refuted, it has generated considerable commentary. Some left-wing authors argue that since the administration had in fact always been "right wing," no such ideological shift occurred. But if this is true, why was the administration slow in beginning disincorporation and why did it apply its program to relatively unimportant entities? A right-wing government would logically undertake an ambitious program from the beginning of the administration, as happened in England under Margaret Thatcher. And it would not continuously stress the state's "governance" of economic activity and declare that "this is not a privatization process."[43]

The denationalization explanation. Denationalization is the explanation commonly accepted by both the academic and political left. They
see the disincorporation process as the handing over of the national
patrimony to the capitalists, a privatization program inspired, if not
imposed, by the International Monetary Fund (IMF).

This explanation has some weaknesses. The sale of state enterprises
has been substantially less far-reaching than officially claimed. Most
disincorporations were merely formal closures of inoperative trust
funds. Further, some of the disincorporated entities had been in liquidation for years. This hypothesis also cannot explain the sale of several
companies to official unions. Cases in point are Bicicletas Cóndor,
Grupo Industrial Cadena, and some small textile companies. As for IMF
influence, the fund obviously supports such a policy, but that is not to
say that it imposed the program.

This hypothesis raises another point regarding the government's
vulnerability to pressures, from both the private sector and foreign institutions. As noted above, when the government's economic position
was most precarious, in 1982 and 1983, it did not bow to these pressures.
Why then would it do so two years later, when it was in a relatively
improved situation?

**The restoration of the government–private sector partnership as an
explanation.** This interpretation, based on elements of political economy, notes that a distinctive feature of Mexico's development model for
over three decades—from 1940 to 1970—was the partnership between
the government and the business community within a "corporatist"
arrangement. Politics was reserved for the "political class" (the party in
power), while the economy was reserved for the private sector. By tacit
agreement, neither interfered with the other.[44]

The erratic and ill-fated economic policy pursued under Luis
Echeverría (1970–1976) led, however, to growing discontent within the
private sector. Moreover, one of the keystones of Echeverría's economic
policies, the active expansion of the state in the economic arena, severely
strained the relationship between the public and private sectors. Toward the end of Echeverría's term, the business community created the
Business Coordinating Council (Consejo Coordinador Empresarial, or
CCE) to present a unified front against what they perceived as an attack
on private enterprise.

Then came the oil boom, which helped heal the rift between the public and private sectors. Oil revenues flowed in at levels sufficient to finance
both sectors. The economy was on the fast track.

With the 1982 crisis, however, private sector doubts reappeared about the government's ability to manage the economy. The head-on collision came in September 1982, when President José López Portillo announced the nationalization of Mexican banks.[45] The private sector responded with a demand for "new rules of the game," involving less state intervention in economic life. Citing the economic crisis as proof of the government's incompetence as economic manager, private sector organizations demanded a redefinition of the public and private sectors' roles in the economy and in society.

One of de la Madrid's first official tasks was to reestablish the dialogue with the private sector, in the midst of the worst economic crisis Mexico had faced in over half a century. He also inherited from López Portillo two unresolved problems stemming from the bank nationalization. The first was what to do with the shares of over four hundred companies in which the banks held minority or majority interest. The second problem was how to structure Mexico's new financial sector. Before the nationalization, a multiple banking system that integrated banking, insurance, real estate, and brokerage functions had emerged. Through the nationalization, the government had acquired de facto ownership of a complex financial system.[46]

All private sector organizations backed the former bank owners' demand for indemnification for all banks and the return of insurance companies, real estate firms, brokerages, etc. They sought, in other words, to retain the right to participate as nonbanking financial intermediaries. The government agreed to return the nonbanking companies and set to calculating the indemnification package for bank assets, despite conflicting views within the government as to whether the private sector should play any role in nonbanking financial intermediation.

On the economic front, the severity of the crisis led the government to adopt an "orthodox" austerity program in 1983, projected to last for two years—through 1984—after which the economy would be on a steady growth path once again. Although this program had the support of the business community, it did not address the real sources of conflict between the public and private sectors. After long and difficult negotiations, the government agreed in the second half of 1984 to allow private participation in nonbanking financial institutions and returned to former bankers some of their most profitable businesses. But the rest of the private sector remained suspicious of government. Nothing had changed to guarantee that actions similar to the bank nationalization would not happen again in the future. For many, the basic problem was political, since an unchecked executive could theoretically take action against private sector interests at any time. Businesses continued to demand smaller government and repeal of the constitutional amendments introduced by de la Madrid.

The 1985 congressional elections were fast approaching, and Mexico's political climate was uneasy, aroused by important opposition advances in the elections of 1983. Throughout the two years of economic austerity, the business community had been outspoken on both economic and political affairs. During this same period, the government announced its intention to open up the economy and to join the General Agreement on Tariffs and Trade, initiating talks with the GATT in 1984. Both plans met strong opposition from several quarters of private industry. How could the government achieve its objectives without alienating the private sector, whose cooperation was vital in the effort to reinvigorate the economy?

At the beginning of 1985, major political and economic obstacles for the Mexican government loomed on horizon. The common denominator in all of these was the business community. If the private sector continued making political inroads, or if it questioned the validity of the 1985 election results, the second half of de la Madrid's term (1985–1988) would not be smooth, and the economy would most certainly continue to stagnate without renewed private investment.

Against this backdrop, it seems no coincidence that the first disincorporation package was announced in February 1985. The announcement was met with skepticism regarding the government's real intentions and the extent of its commitment to implement the program. By mid-1985, the main economic indicators signaled that the economic crisis was far from resolved and was, in fact, worsening. After two years of economic stagnation and high inflation (though lower than 1982 levels), the government lacked credibility and the opposition seemed to be gaining strength. Nevertheless, the government won the 1985 congressional elections by a landslide, although there were numerous charges of electoral fraud in the northern states.

A few months later, oil prices collapsed and the economy relapsed into high inflation and recession. The government accelerated the disincorporation process, and this time around the program met with a notably changed private sector attitude. The private sector now strongly supported government measures to handle the economic crisis.[47] It seems clear that the government's main reason for implementing and accelerating the disincorporation process was its need to resume the old public-private partnership in order to stem the growing political activism of business and to secure business support for the administration's other economic policies.[48]

Several factors argue in favor of this hypothesis. First, things were not moving in the right direction. The government had been unable to regain private sector trust, and every day brought new challenges to government legitimacy. Some key government programs to deal with the declining economy failed to command the support of the business sector. Furthermore, demands for privatization were growing louder.

Second, the disincorporation policy was not a "social demand." That is, no group outside the business community or official party sector had demanded the policy.[49]

Third, the disincorporation process has been ill defined and sometimes contradictory. There has been no comprehensive announcement of a full-fledged program, only partial announcements of limited lists of entities slated for disincorporation, and these same entities frequently reappeared in later lists.

The auction process the government has followed when selling enterprises to the private sector has created two additional problems. First, losing bidders have been highly critical of the government's selection process—carried out behind closed doors—in which the winner is often not the top bidder, since the government also considers other factors such as competition, guarantee of investments, and the like. This was the case in the sale of the forestry company Atenquique.

The second problem is that, in most sales, the only bidders have been large industrial conglomerates, large individual investors, or the most powerful labor unions. Consequently, major privatization operations have resulted in sales to huge private sector investment groups. Enterprises involved in such transactions include Atenquique, Hules Mexicanos, Minera Cananea, and, more recently, the partial sale of Compañía Mexicana de Aviación. The government has not used the disincorporation process to "democratize" capital through the stock exchange or to transfer at least partial ownership of enterprises to their workers. The sale of a few companies to labor unions was a concession to the union leaders rather than to the workers.

From the standpoint of political economy, one can question a procedure that tends to reinforce an already widely unequal distribution of wealth. But from the political viewpoint, it is clear that the government is meeting one of the private sector's principal demands without losing its power to regulate and direct the economy.

The government's disincorporation policy has received the unanimous approval of private sector organizations. One might argue that the private sector's adherence to the December 1987 Economic Solidarity Pact (with the government and labor unions) attests to the effectiveness of the disincorporation process in changing private sector attitudes. Witness the private sector's acceptance of the pact's extensive price controls, a strategy the private sector had resoundingly rejected in the past.

Of the several alternative explanations for the Mexican government's pursuit of a disincorporation strategy, the hypothesis that advances the restoration of the government–private sector partnership appears to enjoy broadest support. In fact, it was not until November 1989, four years after the start of the disincorporation process, that President Carlos Salinas de Gortari in his first State of the Union address, articulated a clear social case for privatization: that the government can, through disincorporation or privatization, conserve fiscal and administrative resources needed for education, health, and social welfare programs.[50]

> The reality is that in Mexico a larger state has resulted in less capacity to respond to the social demands of our fellow citizens and, in the end, greater weakness of the state itself. As the public sector's productive activities grew, its attention to potable water supply, health, rural investment and food supply, housing, the environment, and justice decreased. The size of the state was growing while the well-being of the people was deteriorating. . . . As the facts show, the state concerned itself more with administering its properties than with meeting pressing social needs.[51]

This has become his government's case for the privatization effort in coming years.

Conclusion

This chapter analyzed and evaluated the disincorporation process currently under way in Mexico. A number of hypotheses were advanced to explain its nature and timing, as well as its implications outside the economic sphere. Because this process is still under way, both its evolution over time and the study of as-yet-unexplored issues will go far toward a more comprehensive understanding of this process.

Among the issues to be examined in the future is the creation of government enterprises at the state and local levels—the *paramunicipales*. Information about these entities is still scarce, but there are an estimated 194 *paramunicipales* in the state of Mexico alone.[52] Although these public enterprises exist in only a few states to date, their potential for growth is enormous.

It is difficult to predict the course that disincorporation will follow in the future or how far it will go. And changes in its direction, scope, or intensity may occur under the Salinas administration, although signs seem to indicate that the new government will continue to advance the program. Significantly, the Mexican government now speaks of the dis-incorporation process as a "social demand," in an apparent effort to forestall future criticism of the program.

The Uneasy Steps toward Privatization in Brazil

The wave of sentiment for privatization that has swept much of Latin America in recent years has also reached Brazil. As an idea, privatization has been gathering surprising popularity in many influential segments of Brazilian society. The federal government during the administration of Jose Sarney emphatically reiterated its commitment to this idea and even announced an ambitious, though vague, privatization program. Yet the effective advancement of privatization has been modest.

Notwithstanding the Brazilian government's rhetorical stance in favor of privatization, the actual transfer of public enterprises to the private sector has had, through 1988, little effect on the importance of public production in the Brazilian economy. Even though the relative magnitude of the overall transfers is small, several privatization cases seem to have paved the way for a bolder effort in the near future. In fact, it appears that privatization is bound to become much more important during the next few years in Brazil. This essay examines the case for privatization in the country, considering the specific characteristics of its economy, and analyzes the recent Brazilian experience with privatization, its achievements, shortfalls, and difficulties. It also contemplates the future of privatization in Brazil, its potential, and its limits.

The Case for Privatization in Brazil

Brazil's privatization debate has been strongly influenced by the world-wide privatization movement. Particularly influential have been the Western European experiences, especially the British and French cases. Furthermore, the experience of countries like Spain, which are governed by socialist parties, has softened opposition to privatization in some segments of Brazilian society, undercutting privatization's label as a radical rightist program.

Naturally, some of the classical arguments for privatization that have been important in those countries are being used in the Brazilian debate. But more specific arguments inspired by the present situation of the Brazilian economy have played a preeminent role in that debate. It is useful to review briefly the most important of both kinds of arguments, assessing their forcefulness in the light of the specific characteristics of the Brazilian economy.

The idea that privatization enhances economic efficiency has proved to be very appealing in the Brazilian debate. Nevertheless, in Brazil as in many other countries, it is still very poorly understood that it is the interaction between private property and competition that leads to efficiency. There is a widespread belief that the source of inefficiency lies simply in public ownership. Turning a public monopoly into a private monopoly might not promote economic efficiency, and might even lead to loss of efficiency. Privatization tends to induce productive efficiency, but allocative efficiency may not result if there is no competition in the product markets, no risk of takeover, and a negligible risk of bankruptcy.[1]

The serious financial crisis that the Brazilian public sector faced in the 1980s generated several additional privatization arguments. As also happened elsewhere, privatization has often been erroneously seen in Brazil as a way to reduce the government deficit—and to change accordingly the fiscal stance—by an amount equivalent to the proceeds of the asset sales. The sources of such confusion have been well analyzed in the literature. Because an asset sale produces no change in the net worth position of the public sector, there is no real fiscal impact.[2]

Since the public sector borrowing requirement (PSBR) has been used as a measure of fiscal stance, and since asset sales reduce this requirement, there is a natural temptation to see asset sales as producing a contractionary change in fiscal stance. The problem is that in the case of asset sales—and in many others—the PSBR constitutes a misleading measure of fiscal stance. If the asset sales proceeds were used, for example, to finance a corresponding rise in government consumption, there would be no change in the PSBR. And one would be led to believe that an increase in government consumption financed by public asset sales should not be seen as a change in fiscal stance. The PSBR concept is obtained from an accounting system that does not discriminate between current and capital accounts, as is the usual practice in business accounting, and herein lies the difficulty. In the business world it is a matter of common sense: as long as book values are correct, asset sales should not affects profits or losses.[3]

A related privatization argument popular in Brazil is that the crowding out of the private sector would be avoided if the government stopped issuing bonds and, instead, started selling equity in public enterprises. But if the shares are to be sold in the domestic capital market, this argument also falters. Financing the public deficit implies a demand for capital market resources that may drive up interest rates. In macroeconomic terms, that demand remains constant whether it is met by equity sales or by bond issues. Both involve placing government assets in the private sector. Depending upon the private sector's preferences for one or the other of these two assets, the effects on the interest rate may vary, but in principle one may not say in which case the effect will be greater.[4]

A more elaborate privatization argument regards asset sales as a way to restructure the public sector's consolidated balance sheet, reducing its overindebtedness.[5] This would make the public deficit less dependent on the behavior of both domestic and foreign interest rates. Moreover, whenever private investors could perceive profit opportunities in public sector assets inadequately exploited by the state, they would be inclined to pay for those assets more than the present value of the profit flow that the state would lose by selling them. Under these conditions the sale of such assets could have a positive effect on the public sector's net worth.[6] And government would find it cheaper to finance the deficit by selling those assets than by issuing additional debt.

It is important to know, however, whether the profit opportunities perceived by private investors arise from potential efficiency gains or from the possibility of exploiting existing monopoly power. If the latter is the case, the relief in the public finances would stem from government's having closed its eyes to a loss in allocative efficiency—hardly what the sounder defenders of the connection between privatization and economic efficiency have in mind.[7] It is also important to ask in each situation whether some of the profit opportunities envisaged by private investors are really beyond the public sector's reach. Changes in public pricing policies to correct prices that have obviously lagged behind costs, for example, are certainly not. Often, in Brazil in particular, such situations stem from myopic anti-inflationary price controls. And if prices are supposed to be allowed to rise after privatization, it may be wiser to raise them before that, and then evaluate whether privatization arguments remain relevant for the specific case.

A quite different privatization argument, which likewise stems from the present financial difficulties of the Brazilian public sector, has been insistently defended by Ignácio Rangel, a retired economist of Brazil's national development bank, the Banco Nacional de Desenvolvimento Econômico e Social (BNDES), who happens to be extremely influential among public sector managers. He believes that the development of public utilities is bound to be the catalyst for the next phase of economic growth in Brazil. And he argues that the required investment effort in such a capital-intensive area calls for much greater participation by the private sector. He points out that the old arrangement— which has assigned the maintenance and expansion of public utilities to the state—functioned reasonably well for approximately three decades, but now needs to be replaced. It has led to public sector overindebtedness and inhibited the state's ability to finance much-needed investment in public utilities.

Fortunately, according to Rangel, the Brazilian private sector faces the inverse problem: investment opportunities in areas that have traditionally been left to the private sector are becoming scarce. This leads to a natural solution. Since savings are being generated within the private sector, it is only logical that investment opportunities in public utilities should be opened up to the private sector. This would avoid the difficult and unnecessary financial intermediation strains that are involved in channeling the needed investment funds from the private to the public sector. According to Rangel, most of those strains arise because state-owned enterprises are unable to pledge their fixed assets to creditors as security for the payment of their debt. The creditors know that it is very difficult, if not impossible, to seize those assets when the loans are not properly serviced. This amounts to an elaborate way of saying that the enterprises have lost their creditworthiness.[8]

In the last section below some problems with Rangel's argument will be analyzed. But regardless of how convincing or unconvincing his views on privatization may be, they have had a significant influence on public enterprise managers and top-level public servants. Even though those ideas have not been bought at face value, they have caused a lot of unrest within the public sector.[9] Since he is widely perceived as a leftist and nationalist economist, his stand on the issue has helped lead influential groups within the public sector to view the debate on privatization in Brazil as something more complex than a simple ideological clash.

The view that the overindebtedness of the public sector is hampering much-needed investment in the key sectors of the economy dominated by public enterprises, and that privatization may be the way to resume the expansion of those sectors, is widespread in Brazil today, reaching well beyond Rangel's audience. Many Brazilians share the general idea that present financial constraints on the state constitute a structural impediment to the maintenance of proper investment efforts in those sectors, and that privatization could solve their investment financing problem. In the discussion below, it is argued that there is a problem of macroeconomic inconsistency in this view. Nevertheless, in the case of individual sectors, particularly the smaller ones, privatization may help overcome investment financing difficulties. Privatization is also becoming an attractive idea to public sector managers who are tired of seeing government-approved investment projects slashed in order to keep PSBR under control.[10]

The Recent Brazilian Privatization Experience

Privatization has been mentioned as an explicit public policy objective in Brazil since at least mid-1979, when the government passed legislation on the issue and created the National Program for Public Sector Rationalization.[11] In 1981 new legislation established rules for transferring public enterprises to the private sector.[12] A special tripartite commission, formed by officials from the Ministries of Planning, Finance, and Public Sector Rationalization, was created to manage the privatization process. It was supposed to help the ministries single out the enterprises that could be transferred and submit to the president proposed sale prices and conditions. Foreign investors were legally barred from the privatization process. Furthermore transfer provisions specified that control would not be passed to foreign investors at a later date.

In November 1985, eight months after the end of the military government, new legislation changed privatization procedures, with the creation of the Interministerial Privatization Council, headed by the minister of planning and comprising the ministers of finance, public sector rationalization, industry and commerce, as well as the ministers responsible for the enterprises singled out for privatization.[13] Restrictions on the direct transfer of control to foreign investors were maintained, but conditions barring them from acquiring control later on were dropped. The council was supposed to identify privatization cases following legal guidelines.[14]

In late 1986 procedures were further modified, enhancing the council's executive power.[15] The initiative for and management of the privatization process were taken away from the minister responsible for the enterprise to be transferred and given to the council itself. New operational procedures—established as a means to increase the degree of transparency of the privatization process—involved private consulting and auditing firms, to be selected by BNDES, which was granted a central role in coordinating the operational part of the public asset transfers under the council's supervision.

Notwithstanding efforts to build up the legal and administrative framework for asset sales to the private sector, the effective results of the privatization drive in the period 1980–1986 were extremely modest. Sales proceeds totaled approximately US$190 million. This figure is less than 0.6 percent of the overall net worth of federal public enterprises in December 1985. It was also approximately 1.5 percent of the market value of the federal public enterprises listed on stock exchanges at that time.[16] Only seventeen transfers to the private sector were registered, just one of them after 1984. Table 4.1 lists the transferred enterprises, the manner of sale, and the sale prices.

The modest results, particularly after 1984, led to the legislation that enhanced the power of the Interministerial Privatization Council in late 1986, as noted above. During 1987 four additional enterprises were transferred to the private sector, and the assets of at least one more, which was closed down, were sold to a private firm. Table 4.2 provides a list of the four enterprises involved in the privatization operations concluded in 1987. Additional sales proceeds reached US$27 million.[17] Total proceeds during the 1980–1987 period were, therefore, less than US$220 million.

Most of the enterprises appearing in Tables 4.1 and 4.2 are former private concerns that were absorbed by the public sector when on the verge of bankruptcy. During the 1970s and early 1980s many of them had fallen under the control of BNDES, which came to be known in Brazil as "BNDES hospital." "Hospital stays" often involved extensive and costly restructuring. Privatization proceeds were often less than restructuring costs incurred by BNDES. Other firms in financial distress were absorbed by the treasury and Banco do Brasil. In effect, what has happened so far in Brazil is a reprivatization process, something far different from the transfer to the private sector of enterprises well entrenched in the public sector. The same pattern may be observed in the privatizations concluded in 1988.

Some recent privatization cases illustrate important features of the current privatization process in Brazil. The country's new legal and institutional framework set up in 1985 and 1986 allows for a relatively high flexibility in asset transfers. The manner of sale has varied according to the case. In the transfer of Nova América—a company that had been extensively restructured by BNDES after bankruptcy and that is the largest textile firm in the state of Rio de Janeiro—BNDES's controlling shares

TABLE 4.1   Concluded Privatizations in Brazil, 1980–1986

Enterprise	Ministry or public enterprise group	Industry	Date of privatization	Manner of sale	Operation value in thousands of current US$
Cia. Brasileira de Cimento Portland Perus e Estrada de Ferro Perus-Pirapora e Cibrape[a]	Finance Ministry	Cement	May 20, 1980	Competitive bid	15,879.4
Cia. Quimica do Reconcavo (CQR)	PETROBRAS	Chemicals	Nov. 24, 1981	Direct sale	5,061.0
Cia. America Fabril[b]	PETROBRAS	Textiles	Nov. 31, 1981	Competitive bid	28,756.0
Riocell	Banco do Brasil	Paper pulp	Mar. 10, 1982	Direct sale	77,542.2
Metodo-Organização e Planejamento de Sistemas Empresariais Ltda.	Caixa Econômica Federal	Consulting	June 1, 1982	Direct sale	11.6
Cia. de Tecidos Dona Isabel[b]	Finance Ministry	Textiles	July 1982	Competitive bid	16,897.6
Industria Brasileira de Papel (INBRAPEL)	Finance Ministry	Paper	Aug. 27, 1982	Competitive bid	3,245.3
Cia. Pernambucana de Borracha Sintetica (COPERBO)	PETROBRAS	Synthetic rubber	Dec. 28, 1982	Direct sale	24,771.6
Oleos de Palma Agroindustrial (OPALMA)	SIDERBRAS	Vegetable oils	Mar. 25, 1983	Competitive bid	3,055.5
Cia. Federal de Seguros	Social Security Ministry	Insurance	Apr. 20, 1983	Competitive bid	7,107.3
Nitriflex-Industria e Comercio	PETROBRAS	Chemicals	Apr. 27, 1983	Competitive bid	5,871.8
Livraria Jose Olympio Editora, Encine e Didacta	BNDES	Publishing	Apr. 16, 1984	Auction	218.2
Cia. Melhoramentos de Blumenau (Grande Hotel)	Finance Ministry	Hotel	June 9, 1986	Competitive bid	420.2

Blank cell = not applicable.
a. In the case of this enterprise only fixed assets were sold to the private sector.
b. Re-privatized immediately after falling under state control.
SOURCE: Mendes, "Uma análise do programa brasileiro," and Secretaria de Controle de Empresas Estatais, annual reports.

TABLE 4.2   Concluded Privatizations in Brazil, 1987

Enterprise	Public enter-pise group	Industry	Date of privatization	Manner of sale	Buyer	Operation value in thousands of current US$
Cia. Nacional de Tecidos Nova América S.A.	BNDES	Textiles	June 9, 1987	Auction	Multitextile (Cataguazes-Leopoldina Group)	15,855.7
Máquinas Piratininga do Nordeste S.A.	BNDES	Capital goods	July 23, 1987	Competitive bid	Cimento Portland Poty (Votorantim Group)	1,363.2
Máquinas Piratininga S.A.	BNDES	Capital goods	Sept. 15, 1987	Competitive bid	Wuppertal-Industria oe Maquinas Ltda.	106.6
Ferritas Magneticas S.A. (FERMAG)	CVRD[a]	Magnetic alloys	Nov. 26, 1987	Competitive bid	Araldi Participacoes	n.a.

n.a. = not available.
a. Companhia Vale do Rio Doce.
SOURCE: Conselho Interministerial de Privatização, "Relatório de atividades desenvolvidas."

were auctioned in the Rio de Janeiro stock exchange after a minimum price per share was established.[18]

A different solution was adopted, for example, in the transfer of Máquinas Piratininga do Nordeste, a capital goods producer that had also fallen under BNDES's control. It was sold by tender, after a minimum price was set. Of the three bidders that were prequalified, two were asked to present written offers simultaneously. The highest bid— from the Votorantim Group, the largest industrial conglomerate in the country—was 6.1 percent above the minimum price.[19]

In the first privatization concluded in 1988, an auction was again used to sell BNDES's controlling shares in Eletrosiderúrgica Brasileira (SIBRA), a manganese alloys producer. The shares—comprising 57.6 percent of the voting stocks and 18.4 percent of the company's equity— were sold, at more than four times the minimum price set, to Companhia Paulista de Ferros Ligas, for US$29 million, 20 percent in cash. The remaining 80 percent was financed by BNDES itself. The inflation-indexed debt is to be paid in eight years at an annual real interest rate of 12 percent.[20]

The SIBRA auction illustrates that, so far, privatization in Brazil shows little effective concern with competition and economic efficiency, notwithstanding the explicit concern with productive efficiency.[21] SIBRA's transfer increased the purchaser's share in the manganese alloys market to 85 percent. There were ten other viable bidders to whom the transfer could have been made. Obviously the question of market share and monopoly power did not influence the government's choice.[22] Of course there are difficulties involved in convincing public opinion that public assets may have to be sold below their market value because of considerations of economic efficiency. One solution might be to bar particular groups from the sale process, whenever recommended by such considerations.[23]

The possibility of barring certain candidates from a given transfer case is already established in the present privatization procedures, which may be briefly described as follows.[24] After an enterprise is selected to be transferred to the private sector, a consulting firm—chosen from those registered in the BNDES procurement files—is contracted to closely evaluate the enterprise's problems, as well as to propose restructuring measures to be followed in the privatization process. This might lead to what has been labeled a "previous adjustment program," a procedure that could involve sales of nonoperational assets, asset write-offs, solutions to labor problems, debt rescheduling, or even breaking up of the enterprise. It could also involve changes in marketing and production strategies. Based on the consulting firm's recommendations, the Interministerial Privatization Council's secretary formulates a proposal to be submitted to the council. When the proposal is approved, and if the enterprise is already considered ripe for privatization, the public phase of the transfer starts.

The privatization decision may involve share transfers or direct fixed-asset sales, or a combination of both. The first part of the new phase involves the valuation of the shares and assets to be sold. Again, there is resort to a specialized consulting firm registered in BNDES's procurement files. This firm's work is supposed to be accompanied by an independent audit. After a decision is made on price and conditions, a public announcement is made in the press to identify the bidders. Full disclosure of information about the enterprise is supposed to be granted to all interested buyers. Bidders who are qualified are then publicly asked to participate in the final act of the process, which may involve either an auction or a sale by tender in a public event. Competition and economic efficiency considerations could be taken into account in the qualification process, although hitherto this process has mainly been justified as a means to establish the creditworthiness of the participants before bidding, since a large part of the asset sales has been financed by BNDES.

Seven other enterprises under BNDES's control were scheduled for privatization or closure from May to December 1988.[25] The list includes three enterprises in the paper and pulp industry: Aracruz Celulose, Companhia Guatapará de Papel e Celulose (CELPAG), and Companhia Celulose da Bahia (CCB). It also includes Usiminas Mecânica (USIMEC), a capital goods producer; Companhia Siderúrgica do Nordeste (COSINOR), a relatively small steel producer; and two enterprises in the copper mining and smelting industry, Companhia Brasileira de Cobre (CBC) and Caraíba Metais. There are wide differences not only in the scale of the sales operations but also in the degree of difficulty that may be involved. USIMEC, CBC, and Caraíba were considered to be the most difficult cases. To facilitate matters, Caraíba Metais was broken up into two companies, Caraíba Mineração and Caraíba Metalúrgica, separating the mining from the smelting activities. Only the smelting plant would go through a privatization process.

One of the most interesting recent privatization cases involved Aracruz Celulose, transferred in early May 1988. This large, efficient, and very profitable concern produces almost 500 thousand tons of paper pulp yearly, of which three-fourths have been exported, generating an export revenue of US$200 million in 1987. It is also engaged in a US$1 billion expansion project, largely financed (60 percent) by BNDES itself.[26] Aracruz initially involved an association between the state and private investors, both foreign and Brazilian. A shareholders' agreement subsequently put the enterprise under BNDES control in 1975. Just before the privatization, BNDES held approximately 31 percent of the total equity capital and 41 percent of the voting shares.

A package consisting of 26.2 percent of the company's voting shares—the maximum percentage of voting shares that any individual shareholder may have, according to the prevailing shareholders agreement—was offered for sale to a single buyer, either a sole investor or a group of investors. The agreement also establishes that control of the company is to remain in Brazilian hands. The sale passed control from BNDES to a coalition of private Brazilian shareholders. Nevertheless, the bank remains the company's most important creditor.[27] The transfer of Aracruz to the private sector in 1988 was by far the largest privatization operation in the country up to that time. Eight large Brazilian groups were qualified to participate in the auction. The winner was the Safra Group—controlled by a Lebanese-Brazilian family with strong interests in the banking industry, both in Brazil and abroad—which offered US$133.7 million. Interestingly, the buyer accepted BNDES financing for only half of the sales value, even though the bank offered to finance up to 70 percent. The Safra Group found that it could use alternative, cheaper funds to finance the remainder. The inflation-indexed debt is to be paid in eight years at an annual real interest rate of 12 percent.[28]

Another major privatization operation, concluded in the first semester of 1988, involved CELPAG, also previously controlled by BNDES. This firm is, in fact, an investment project, a paper and pulp factory scheduled to begin operation only in 1991. Although only two bidders participated in the auction, the winning bid was 90 percent over the established minimum price. Two-thirds of the voting shares were sold to the Votorantim Group, already mentioned above, for US$72.7 million. Votorantim also decided not to accept BNDES financing for 70 percent of the sales value, which means that the financing conditions were less favorable than was generally believed.[29]

The Future of Privatization in Brazil

In late March 1988 President Sarney sent a legislative proposal to Congress setting the legal foundation for a significant enhancement of the privatization policy in Brazil, as part of a more general effort to respond to the alarming trends in the public sector deficit. In the previous months the government had been criticized for its apparent lack of commitment to the idea of privatization.[30] If approved by Congress, the new law would allow the president to sell the shares in monopolistic public enterprises that are not strictly needed for the maintenance of control over them. The law would also create the "special class voting share," inspired by the British "golden share" experience. This share would entitle the state to exert a firmer regulating power over the enterprise after privatization, controlling decisions involving pricing and investment policy, for example.[31]

Furthermore, the proposed law would limit the voting power of any shareholder in privatized enterprises to 5 percent of the voting shares. This measure was presented as an incentive for a more dispersed pattern of share ownership. In fact, the law would also permit the president to create additional incentives to foster such a pattern of share ownership, as well as to induce the conversion of public debt (both foreign and domestic) into equity capital in these enterprises.

Getting the new legislation approved by the Congress may prove to be a difficult task. In response to early reactions, the government was compelled in mid-April 1988 to send a different version of the law to the Congress, explicitly stating that the oil company PETROBRAS (but not its subsidiaries) would not be affected.[32] There was also fear among holders of public bonds that the inducement to convert public debt into equity in public enterprises might eventually provide the legal basis for a compulsory swap. The government promptly affirmed that no such measure had been considered.

Some groups are bound to oppose fiercely any attempt to extend privatization to the very core of the public enterprise sector. Management of the enterprises constitutes perhaps the most influential of those groups. Their opposition was strengthened by the fact that in some of the privatizations already completed in Brazil managers have been dismissed.[33] Management has obstructed the privatization process in other countries, as well. Kay and Thompson point out that the privatization pattern in Britain was extensively determined by management's convenience.[34]

Opposition from labor should not be underestimated. Featherbedding has been a problem in some public enterprises, but even in those in which it has not, for the average employee privatization would mean reduced fringe benefits and a higher probability of being dismissed in the future. As in other countries, the Brazilian government has been tempted to win labor and management support for privatization, or at least reduced resistance, by allowing employees to buy shares at discounted prices.[35] Even if all employees were able to buy the offered shares, however, this could be interpreted as a giveaway of public assets to the elite of the Brazilian working class, something hardly justifiable by considerations of distributional equity. The policy is even less justifiable when one takes into account that it is chiefly the top layers of the employees who will be able to buy the shares and, therefore, benefit from the giveaway.

Within both the executive and legislative branches of government, privatization has faced serious opposition from certain segments. Control over public enterprises has been seen as an important source of power by ministers, top public officials, and politicians—power to appoint managers and even employees, power to affect large investment programs and the enterprises' procurement policy, and power to capitalize on successful enterprises or at least on their generally high profile. This clearly undermines a more effective commitment to the advancement of privatization.

Recent experience shows that even marginal advancements may be difficult. So far, as noted, the privatization effort has been concentrated on former private enterprises that had fallen under BNDES control. The bank's management supports privatization of these unsolicited acquisitions because their sale (even if only a fraction is received in cash) would free resources to be allocated elsewhere. Although the privatization effort has consciously followed a path of least resistance, it has often had to face serious political difficulties. A good example is given by the intervention of public actors when the notoriously inefficient Caraíba copper mines were to be closed as part of the restructuring of Caraíba Metais. Fierce opposition to closure on the part of the governor and congressmen of the politically powerful state of Bahia forced the Interministerial Privatization Council to abandon the recommendation for closure.[36] Political difficulties are bound to become much more serious when the easier reprivatization phase is over.

The pace and the limits of privatization in Brazil will also be shaped by strict economic constraints, which are bound to impose difficulties quite different from those stemming from vested interests and political opposition. Privatization represents a structural change that has to be justified by long-term policy objectives. Brazil's primary long-run economic goal today is the resumption of growth. From 1940 to 1980, Brazil sustained an average annual growth rate above 7 percent, but in the 1981–1987 period the rate fell to only 2.9 percent. The effective advancement of privatization in Brazil will be determined by the extent to which this process fosters or hinders rapid and sustained economic growth.

It is true that, as part of a more general effort to reform and modernize the public sector and to enhance economic efficiency, privatization might contribute significantly to the resumption of economic growth.[37] But the Brazilian economy will not be able to attain again the high average annual growth rates of the past without a sizable increase in its present investment ratio. And this poses important questions about the economy's ability to finance the required additional investment effort and about whether privatization may make that financing easier or more difficult.

As seen above, the case for privatization in Brazil has been made partly in terms of the positive effects it could have on investment financing, particularly in sectors controlled by public enterprises. As Rangel and others have argued, given the serious financial difficulties permeating the public sector, transferring capital-intensive public enterprises to the financially unconstrained private sector would be the natural way to increase much-needed investment in those enterprises and raise aggregate investment. The problem with this argument is that it lacks macroeconomic consistency. There is an aggregate savings constraint to be faced. Shifting investment responsibility from the public to the private sector will not lead to a higher and sustainable overall investment ratio unless aggregate savings are increased accordingly.

Once this is properly understood, one is led to a quite different discussion, which centers on the present determinants of the savings constraint in the Brazilian economy. Since the mid-1970s, the domestic aggregate savings ratio in Brazil has fallen by nearly a third. Most economists agree that the fall was the result of the asymmetrical adjustment pattern of the Brazilian economy in response to the external shocks in the late 1970s and early 1980s. Various factors interacted to place most of the adjustment burden on the public sector.[38] The required adjustment within the public sector itself led to the elimination of its savings generation capacity. In the mid-1970s a third of domestic savings was generated by the public sector.

If the Brazilian economy is to again sustain a high growth rate it must enhance the present low domestic savings effort significantly. Designing a policy that could provide that enhancement involves some important trade-offs, which have been analyzed through simulations based on simple consistency models.[39] These simulations outline the required increase in private sector savings under different scenarios using distinct sets of hypotheses about the evolution of income distribution and variables that determine the public sector's savings capacity. The results stress the lack of realism of savings policies that do not restore the importance of public sector savings. This becomes particularly clear with scenarios that involve even a modest and highly probable redistribution of income in favor of labor in the near future, with its consequent impact on the private savings ratio.

If the required additional aggregate savings are to come primarily from the increase in public sector savings, public sector investment is bound to become less financially constrained. Public equity capital would again finance a large part of public enterprises' investment. But in this case, from the strict viewpoint of public investment financing, there would be no reason for privatization. Of course, other arguments may still justify privatization. Yet investment financing constraints are bound to pose difficulties to the advancement of privatization, particularly in the capital-intensive public utilities sector, quite contrary to the arguments of Rangel and others.

If the Brazilian economy manages to resume its historical growth rate, the rapid expansion that will be needed in the public utilities sector will require a significant investment effort. Discussions about the private sector's financial absorptive capacity in privatization programs has usually centered on stocks, as opposed to flows, and on whether the private sector would be able to buy the transferred assets and pay what they are worth. Such discussions are relevant, but it is at least as important to discuss the privatized enterprises' financial ability to maintain the required investment effort in their respective sectors. In capital-intensive sectors, such as electricity, telecommunications, and railroads, even the largest Brazilian corporate groups would face serious difficulties maintaining the required investment effort. Of course, expansion could be extensively financed by the state, as happened in the past in many sectors. But in this case, the argument for privatization would lose force. Furthermore, the large-scale channeling of required public funds into private enterprises may also pose difficulties, already observed in the past, if giveaways are to be avoided and the private character of the enterprises preserved.[40]

The need to avoid giveaways of public funds and assets may prove to be a strong impediment to the asset transfers. Significant giveaways were possible in the 1970s, under the military government, but obvious considerations of distributional equity would tend to make them much more difficult in today's political circumstances. If giveaways are to be avoided, even top public officials involved in the Brazilian privatization program acknowledge that it would be difficult to sell the control of most largest public enterprises.[41] To overcome those difficulties, the government has been considering an alternative privatization strategy. Instead of selling the enterprise to a controlling group, the state would sell shares to a very large number of investors. The maximum voting power of any shareholder would be limited to 5 percent of the voting shares, and the state would maintain a single "golden" share, as described above.[42] This so-called dispersed-ownership model has two problems. First, it may disguise a giveaway of public assets. The explicit rationale of this alternative is that the voting shares would be cheaper than they would be if the enterprise were sold to a controlling group.[43] Second, the effective shelter provided to managers against takeovers may well foster inefficiency.[44]

The private sector's ability to absorb the assets to be transferred as well as to maintain the required investment effort in the privatized sectors will, in some measure, depend on the role allowed foreign investors. Speculation about this raises difficult questions about the relative power of the nationalist coalition within Congress. The potential role of foreign debt-equity conversions also has to be properly considered. But this has been explored elsewhere.[45]

Argentine Privatization in Retrospect

Argentina's recent privatization experience has been influenced by
three factors: the relationship between the parastatal sector and the
larger economy, the way in which the privatization program has been
organized, and official perceptions of the process. Despite the efforts of
the government of Raúl Alfonsín, privatization during its term effected
few actual transfers to the private sector. This chapter argues that this
incomplete privatization resulted from indecision or inability to sell on
the part of the government and a lack of interest within the private
sector, not from ideology or lack of a comprehensive plan. The government's lack of action, in turn, stemmed from legal, political, and
labor problems, while the private sector's inaction was chiefly the result
of economic factors, especially economic stagnation exacerbated by foreign debt.

The basic foundations for a more effective process of privatization
were laid during the first months of President Carlos Saúl Menem's
administration. Although it is too early to evaluate these efforts fully, it
is evident that much ground has been covered in a short period of time.
Foes of privatization are actively opposing the course initiated by the
new administration. These foes are found not only in the unions and
state-owned enterprises, but also in major political parties—including

Menem's own Partido Justicialista—as well as in some large corporations that have profited in their deals with the government.

The lack of strong ideological support for privatization may mean that the forces arrayed against specific transfers can prevent acceleration of privatization overall. However, the fiscal crisis and recent interest in increasing efficiency by redistributing resources may improve prospects for privatization. The need to increase competitiveness internationally remains a strong argument in favor of new privatizations.

Composition of the Parastatal Sector

The wide variety of enterprises in Argentina's parastatal sector offers multiple candidates for privatization. An exhaustive inventory extends the definition of public companies from those in which the government holds majority or minority ownership to those in which the government exerts control over decision making. The productive assets of the public sector, which totaled more than three hundred parastatals in 1985, are classified by institutional category in Table 5.1.

In addition to the companies in Table 5.1, which are defined under statute as public, the state controls many other assets, including rural property belonging to the national government and the military, urban real estate acquired by the central bank through debt settlements, miscellaneous assets (including shareholdings in other firms) belonging to other official banks, idle land in the hands of state companies, especially the railways, and subsurface oil and other mineral reserves. Viewed by industrial sector, the parastatal sector comprises

- national, provincial, and municipal banks

- public utility monopolies

- service companies competing with the private sector

- companies producing "strategic" goods

- companies transferred to the public sector to prevent their collapse

Assigning a monetary value to this property would provide a backdrop against which to evaluate privatization efforts made to date. However, the most notable feature of state enterprises is their lack of transparency. Public administrators have a stake in covering up the assets they administer

TABLE 5.1   Public Sector Enterprises and Productive Assets in Argentina, 1985

Institutional classification	Number of organizations
Decentralized organisms	97
National	20
Provincial	72
Municipal	5
State enterprises	30
National	7
Provincial	23
Mixed companies	9
National	8
Provincial	1
Sociedades anónimas, with the state as majority shareholder	26
National	20
Provincial	6
Sociedades anónimas, with majority or total state control	17
National	8
Provincial	9
State corporations	30
National	9
Provincial	19
Municipal	2
Interstate corporations	9
Interprovincial	4
Binational	5
CAP (meat packing operations)	1
National	1
Radio and TV stations	85
National	39
Provincial	46

SOURCE: Author.

since these assets may confer more power than that ascribed by law to the positions these administrators hold.

The Alfonsín Record

The organizational structure of privatization under Alfonsín. The first privatization-related move of the Radical party after it assumed power in December 1983 was the formation of Commission 414 to manage the government's privatization efforts. The commission comprised representatives from government banks and ministries. Placed under the jurisdiction of the secretary-general of the executive branch, the commission was far removed from public enterprises. The first stage of privatization involved only companies that had become public enterprises when the state rescued them from bankruptcy. One of these—the Siam conglomerate—is analyzed in detail below.

Progress in privatization, however, lagged behind government goals, leading the administration to establish the Ministry of Growth Promotion on July 24, 1985, under the direction of Manuel Tanoira, a private businessman and not a Radical party member. The ministry attempted to stimulate private sector activity in areas that were traditionally reserved for the public sector, but for which the state could no longer provide the needed human and financial resources. The ministry promoted private sector participation in communications, transportation, and general infrastructure, but its efforts met strong resistance from those whose interests were affected and from the most traditional sectors of the Radical party. The lack of support from other areas of the government led Tanoira to resign in January 1986, having implemented none of the privatization projects he had promoted.

Toward the end of 1986, another organization with responsibility in the privatization area came into being—the Directorio de Empresas Públicas (DEP), under the jurisdiction of the Ministry of Public Works and Services. Its explicit objective was to study the principal public enterprises and suggest ways to improve their operating efficiency or recommend privatization. It did not specifically mention privatization but spoke of incorporating private capital into the provision of public services, a role previously reserved for state companies. New attempts to activate the "privatization of growth" strategy were made while the studies were being conducted, but these also were unsuccessful because of opposing interests.

In February 1987 the Ministry of Growth Promotion was phased out and the real decision-making center shifted to the Ministry of Public Works and Services, which shared decision making with DEP and the Ministry of the Economy. Unfortunately, the three agencies were in continual disagreement and thus unable to undertake any concerted privatization activities. The power struggle between the Ministry of Public Works and Services, the Ministry of the Economy, and DEP reached new heights during the difficult days preceding the elections of 1987, when Alfonsín's hopes for reelection hung in the balance.

To resolve the conflict, additional responsibilities were transferred to the Ministry of Public Works and Services, creating the conditions needed to modernize public enterprises and to implement many of the recommendations of previous studies. By 1988 decisions about public enterprises and privatization were made jointly by the Ministry of Public Works and Services and DEP, working in harmony. They made notable progress, including the signing of letters of intent to privatize Aerolíneas Argentinas and Empresa Nacional de Telecomunicaciones (ENTEL). Meanwhile, the privatization topic matured ideologically, and the power of decision passed to those who hold the companies to be privatized (the ministry itself). If one lesson has been learned from the privatization experiences of the past few years, it is that whoever directs the process must put it into effect: in the case of Siam, the comptroller-liquidator, and in the case of the airline Austral Líneas Aéreas, the Ministry of Public Works and Services.

Official Perceptions

How official perceptions of privatization have evolved over the past few years and what obstacles still block the privatization process in Argentina are reflected in the opinions of policy makers responsible for decisions in the area of privatization during Alfonsín's administration. Roque Carranza, minister of public works and services during the early years of the Radical administration, expresses the prevalent opinion toward privatization in 1984–1985:

> The question of how to obtain funds for investment credits or public investments is a point of primary importance. Here privatization may serve as an instrument of growth. If private capital is willing to invest in existing productive activities in areas where security does not demand the present degree of state participation, the revenues realized can be directed toward new investments with higher priority.

Perceptions changed drastically after 1985. Tanoira, the new minister of growth promotion recommended the sale of public entities to the private sector, not as an engine of growth but as a means of survival. Privatization was viewed as essential if Argentina was to escape its persisting economic crisis. As long as the state retained control of inefficient companies, the crisis would continue and perhaps even worsen, quality of services would continue to drop, and essential investments would not be forthcoming. Others in the Alfonsín administration reaffirmed the view that privatization should not be viewed as a threat to Argentina's sovereignty or national principles, but rather as an instrument to guarantee the country's well-being.

TABLE 5.2   Companies Reprivatized in Argentina during 1982–1987

Company	Date	No. of offers	Buyer	Price (thousands of US$)
Siam				
Servicios Asistencial	Dec. 1985	2	Sedimed	275
División Siat (steel pipes)	Feb. 1986	3	Comatter	12,360
Electromecánica	Aug. 1986	2	Sade	2,866
Electrodoméstica	Dec. 1986	1	Aurora	1,642
Lagos del Sur (Sol Jet)	Apr. 1986	6	Centrex	715
Opalinas Hurlingham	June 1986	2	Ind. del Vidrio Plano	1,077
Austral Líneas Aéreas S.A.	Dec. 1987	2	Cielos del Sur	12,800

SOURCE: Author.

Companies Privatized under Alfonsín

All companies transferred to the private sector since 1983, like those divested under the military government from 1976 to 1982, were previously private; they had been taken over by the state when they became insolvent. The Banco Nacional de Desarrollo (BANADE), the national development bank, had acquired stock interest in firms privatized through 1982 when they were unable to pay back loans advanced by the bank. Companies returned to the private sector after 1982 were those in which other government credit institutions had acquired an equity interest, under more or less the same circumstances. It is, then, more fitting to speak of these as *reprivatizations*. Companies reprivatized between 1982 and 1987 appear in Table 5.2. With the exception of Siam Servicios Asistencial and Lagos del Sur, which were paid for in cash, the transactions involved, on average, a 20 percent down payment with the balance due in twelve biannual installments.

Through 1988, revenues from these reprivatizations totaled less than US$32 million, in an economy with a GNP of US$70 billion. Moreover, privatization touched only 4 of the 305 companies in which the state holds total or majority interest.

In each case, the process of privatization is controlled by the ministry or other administrative organization on which the individual company depends. The means of privatization include

- the sale of all or part of the corporation's capital stock

- the sale of company assets in operation, either as a unit to one buyer or to two or more buyers

- the sale of all or part of the assets belonging to nonfunctioning firms, to one or more buyers

Privatization occurs through national or international bidding, according to the terms established in each case. There is broad freedom for disposing of assets, transforming companies, and renegotiating contracts, with preference given to bidders who already own part of the social capital of the company up for sale.

Ministries and other supervisory organizations that preside over public enterprises set the terms for the sales, taking into account the value established by official banks or other appropriate public organizations. The executive branch can allow deferred collection of credits that official organizations have extended to establishments to be privatized.

Austral Líneas Aéreas. Austral Líneas Aéreas, the private Argentinian carrier, went bankrupt and was taken over by the state in 1979. Eight years passed before the company was reprivatized. In debates on air transportation policy from 1983 to 1985, supporters of nonprivatization contended that there was not enough room in the Argentine air transportation industry for two airlines and that it would be best if Austral were absorbed by Aerolíneas Argentinas. Privatization was not yet a declared government objective, and pro-state sectors of the Radical party dominated the decision-making process.

Not until September 1986 was the order issued transferring Austral to the private sector by national bidding. The decree authorizing a fifteen-year concession on the routes Austral had been operating was not issued until two months later, though it was an indispensable requirement for privatization to move ahead. Two private companies were competing in the bidding in October 1987, when complications arose concerning warranties with McDonnell Douglas for three planes under lease to Austral. McDonnell Douglas's request that the original government warranty be replaced by a new one covering the privatized company provoked argument between the bidders and delayed the legal settlement.

The matter of guarantees made the whole process more expensive for both bidding companies, thus reducing their final offers. Both agreed that the government should not have given McDonnell Douglas so much power of decision since the company had an obvious interest in favoring the bidder who would decide to purchase new equipment. Other problems arose regarding the inventory of spare parts. Both of these difficulties, together with the delay in granting the concession on routes, revealed the inexperience of those involved in the privatization procedure. According to private sector participants, these uncertainties and the lack of a reliable regulatory environment interacted to depress bids for the company.

In addition, there was resistance from the company's representatives, who would lose power with privatization and had no incentive for seeing the transfer through to a successful conclusion. Compounding the errors was a lack of understanding of why Austral was being privatized—essentially because the government needed to display effective accomplishments in an area where many declarations had been made but little had been achieved.

Opalinas Hurlingham. The privatization of Opalinas Hurlingham was ordered in February 1985, but its transfer to the private sector was not completed until two years later. BANADE was to manage the transaction, representing the Ministry of Health and Social Services and the two ministries holding shares in Opalinas (Economy and Labor). Nevertheless, other organizations participated in the process. For example, Commission 414 issued the report setting the sale price and sent the tender proposal to the Ministry of Health and Social Services.

Siam S.A. Siam, transferred to the state in the 1970s, comprised four different ventures in 1985: Electromecánica (electromechanics), Electrodoméstica (home appliances), Servicios Asistencial (medical assistance), and Siat (steel pipes). The conglomerate was among a number of companies earmarked in 1977 for privatization through BANADE. The first and second calls for bids, in July and December 1980, elicited no offers.

In August 1981, efforts to sell the ventures separately—without liabilities, in operating condition, and including the transfer of personnel to the buyers—also failed for various reasons: there were no offers for the electromechanics plant; offers for Siat did not comply with bidding terms; the bid for Siam Servicios Asistencial contained flaws; and although the formal offer for Electrodoméstica was prepared, the actual bidding did not take place.

Siam's privatization was reinitiated in 1984 with BANADE in charge of the proceedings. But in December of that year a functionary was charged by the state to order transference of the company's material and nonmaterial assets. In July 1985, bids were requested for the four companies but with the terms of transfer varying by company. At this stage, two fundamental changes had taken place: the initiative was no longer in the hands of a big organization like BANADE but in those of a single person devoted specifically to this task; and the sale was not treated as a single package but as four different companies.

The pace picked up substantially at that point. The first auction— for the medical assistance company—took place in September 1985. A bid from Sedimed for US$275,000 was approved a month later, and in December the company was handed over to the buyer. The second bidding process for a company in the Siam group was organized for the Siat company. Four bids were received in the November 1985 auction, one of which was approved two months later. The buyer, Comatter, paid US$12.4 million for the firm, and the transfer of the company with its 714 employees was effected in February 1986.

The first call for bids for the electromechanical division, in August 1985, failed to attract any bids. The following November brought approval for a new bidding session, and Sade's bid for US$2.9 million was approved and accepted in July 1986. The company, then employing 758 workers, was turned over to the buyer one month later. The home appliances division was put on the block in November 1985, but it too failed to attract any bidders. A second auction was approved in July of the following year, when the company was sold to Electrodomésticos Aurora, the sole bidder, for US$1.6 million. The transfer was completed in December 1986.

Before its privatization, Siam had cost the national treasury around US$15 million per year—despite the fact that the company paid neither taxes nor social security. The four divisions had a combined work force of 2,600 people—mostly elderly—but because of a shortage of working capital, the companies operated at only 30 percent capacity.

Two years after privatization, all the companies were operating at full capacity, paying taxes (US$2.4 million in 1987) and social security, and covering their biannual installments (adjusted for inflation, and with an annual interest rate of 8 percent). The total number of employees increased, although there were cases, such as Siat, where attractive indemnities were paid to workers wishing to leave the company, thus reducing the work force. (Table 5.3 describes the evolution of the Siat company.) During this same period, take-home salaries rose 100 percent in real terms over preprivatization levels.

New technology and organizational improvements stimulated Siat's increased production levels. In one product line, output before

TABLE 5.3	Siat Employment and Production Levels in Argentina, 1984–1988				
Year	1984	1985	1986	1987	1988[a]
Production of steel pipe (tons)	25,000	17,000	7,000	162,000	171,000
Work force	n.a.	n.a.	714	n.a.	884

n.a. = not available.
a. estimated.
SOURCE: Author.

privatization was 60 kilometers of pipe per month; the privatized company was producing 105 kilometers of pipe per month in 1988 with the same work force and operating schedule. In the medical assistance division, the doctors who purchased the company increased the number of beds and set up an intensive therapy unit.

When all payments are received, the sale of the four companies and the other Siam properties will yield about US$30 million. Nevertheless, the Siam privatization process was not devoid of obstacles.

The first major obstacle was union opposition, present from the outset, which claimed that privatization went against the "national interest." Union pressure forced the new purchasers to continue the main activities of each division, with only a few exceptions. Purchasers were also obligated to maintain the plants' locations until the total sale price had been paid—or for a minimum term of eighteen months if the buyers had paid cash. The purchasers also promised to maintain for at least twelve months 80 percent of the employed personnel who were covered by collective work contracts.

A second hurdle was posed by the methods used to establish and index the base value of the businesses. In the first attempts to privatize, these methods rendered sale of the whole conglomerate impossible. Dividing the company into separate units and assigning a more realistic value, adapted to market realities, was therefore a prerequisite for divestiture. Complicating the picture further, public officials feared that they might face legal repercussions if they sold companies for less than the "actual value" of their assets. Most assets controlled by state-managed companies are overvalued on the books, and operating losses tend to push the realistic sales value of parastatals considerably below the nominal value carried on the balance sheets. Bookkeeping values higher than those set by the market exposed officials to criticism from opponents of privatization who accused them of corruption and complicity with the purchasers. The legal mechanism hit upon to overcome this difficulty transferred ultimate responsibility to the president or to Congress; but either recourse, though effective for shielding privatization functionaries from legal action, simply opened the door to additional interference and delays.

Business leaders proved to be an obstacle as well, when they endeavored to persuade the government to sweeten its offers of enterprises with future state contracts, subsidized loans from official banks, and similar concessions. To maintain the integrity of the privatization program, however, the government ultimately resisted these demands.

The nonviability of the home appliances division constituted another obstacle. With a work force of seven hundred employees and a sluggish market for its output, this subdivision would have been unsalable had it been offered on the same basis as the other Siam subdivisions. Accordingly, the state paid indemnities to workers willing to leave, reducing the payroll by two hundred workers.

Results of Privatization through the Alfonsín Years

Argentina's recent privatization experiences are limited to the sale of industrial or utility companies that were previously private. These privatizations did not result from an overall government belief in the expediency of transferring productive assets to the private sector, nor did they spring from convictions about the advantages of deregulation that privatization implies. The sales responded to practical case-by-case advantages and to isolated pressure. The absence of an intense ideological argument had one positive and one negative aspect. On the positive side, if an ideological discussion had started, it would still be going on and nothing would have been sold. The negative aspect is that, lacking an ideological base, each privatization effort fell under attack by interest groups opposing privatization.

Perhaps the most important criterion on which the Argentine government based its decisions was circumstance. The need to transfer goods to the private sector reflected fiscal concerns more than an effort to reassign resources to make them more productive. Besides, in the cases discussed above, the basic decision to sell had been made many years before; delays signaled government impotence. The drive toward privatization gained momentum only when the government realized that these initiatives would confer a positive image. The public wanted concrete accomplishments; the government was determined to provide them. Witness the plethora of promises to privatize and the publicity devoted to the few concrete examples.

The private sector, never much interested in the privatization process, presented few offers for companies to be sold. The sales' main attraction was the financing. As much as 95 percent of the amount privatized could be paid over a period of six years, with state financing providing for 80 percent of the total. Considering that the cost of this financing was equal to the inflation adjustment, and that real interest rates in Argentina in 1988 oscillated between 30 and 50 percent annually, we may conclude that effective sale prices were lower than those formally agreed upon.

Each auction attracted bidders from other industrial sectors, who viewed privatizations as an opportunity to diversify. This is important in an economy like that of Argentina where business purchases or mergers are infrequent. Other interested parties saw the opportunity to

TABLE 5.4   Bank Branches Offered for Sale by Argentina's Central Bank, 1987–1988

	First bidding (Dec. 29, 1987)	Second bidding (Feb. 10, 1988)	Third bidding (Mar. 23, 1988)
Banks offered	50	60	51
Banks sold	34	48	37
Base value (millions of US$) (1)	2.4	2.1	2.3
Sale value (millions of US$) (2)	5.1	7.6	6.8
Ratio of (2) to (1)	2.11	3.62	2.9

SOURCE: Author.

consolidate their presence in the sector by acquiring a well-known company without unmanageable problems and with profitable assets.

Privatization in the Financial Sector

The Argentine financial sector has been in crisis since the beginning of the 1980s, creating problems of solvency and liquidity and forcing the adoption of severe financial measures. The central bank liquidated a number of financial entities and, in the process, acquired their varied assets. When the central bank began to reprivatize these assets, it encountered legal obstacles to their return to the private sector.

At the end of 1987, the central bank decided to sell 147 branches that belonged to liquidated banks. Results of the first three biddings are shown in Table 5.4.

The bidding procedure was limited to nationally owned private banks. The central bank awarded the sale to the highest bidder, who had to agree to return deposits still owed depositors at the time of transfer and to handle the branch's loan portfolios for one year. Payments were in cash or financed through a branch's property.

Starting in mid-1985, the central bank pushed the sale of a wide range of goods it acquired from liquidated financial entities, including real estate, fixed assets, and vehicles. Results of this privatization effort appear in Table 5.5.

The sale or merger of entire financial entities constituted the third and most common aspect of the reprivatization program. Two patterns arose in the sale of functioning, salvageable entities. The first involved mergers agreed upon among the parties and approved—and sometimes supported by—the central bank. Examples are the absorption of Banco Ganadero by Banco Río or of Banco de Crédito Rural Argentino by Banco Financiero Argentino.

TABLE 5.5	Assorted Assets Offered for Sale by Argentina's Central Bank, 1985–1987					
	Real estate		Fixed assets		Vehicles	
	No. of assets	US$ millions	No. of assets	US$ millions	No. of assets	US$ millions
July–Dec. 1985	444	10.4	5,594	0.4	37	0.1
1986	584	26.9	17,587	1.6	38	0.2
1987	668	16.8	13,767	1.6	56	0.4
Total	1,696	54.1	36,948	3.6	131	0.7
SOURCE: Author.						

The second type of sale involved public bidding for banks taken over and restructured by the central bank, which were then merged with the buyer. This procedure governed the absorptions of Banco Internacional by Bank of America; Banco Delta by Banco Río; Banco del Interior y Buenos Aires and Banco Denario by Banco Palmares; Banco Español by Banco Comerical de Norte; and Banco de Italia by Banca Nazionale del Lavoro.

The terms of these operations differed greatly. Besides variations in price, there were different terms of payment, different forms of financing, and different facilities provided by the central bank to the purchasers. The latter included suspension of certain limits and technical relationships (such as financial ratios) and the waiver or deferral of assorted charges. The central bank granted facilitating loans and liquidated certain assets and liabilities.

Theoretically, the central bank sales might not be considered privatizations, as they constitute part of the bank's duties as a comptroller of the system. However, the bank's decision not to merge these liquidated banks with official banks is a positive sign of this institution's recent evolution, reinforced by its decision to sell Banco de Italia, which belonged to Argentine shareholders, to a foreign group.

Obstacles to Privatization

Why was so little achieved in the area of privatization in Argentina during Alfonsín's presidency? The two reasons, offered earlier, are the government's inability or unwillingness to act and the private sector's ambivalence toward the entire privatization process.

An inadequate legal framework. One factor contributing to the government's inability to act was the lack of an adequate legal framework.

Although there is general agreement among the parties involved that the legal framework was not to blame for the scant results, it was not a positive element in the process.

Several legislative proposals were presented to amend the laws that affect privatization, although none were enacted by Congress until President Menem's Enabling Law in 1989. One of these proposals, announced in 1985, features a new mode of private ownership of companies—the Program of Shared Property—through which employees could participate in the purchase of the enterprise. Seniority and salary would determine the level at which an employee could participate, and payment would be generated by a lien on the shares. Once the shares were paid for, an employee could dispose of them at will. Until that time, however, the shares would be managed collectively through a shareholders' organization.

In 1986 another proposal was presented, this time in collaboration with the Ministry of the Economy. The legislation constitutes the most important and up-to-date document concerning privatization, although at the time of this writing its enactment is by no means assured.[1] It authorizes the executive branch to name companies subject to privatization, with some exceptions in "strategic sectors"—such as banking, transportation, communications, natural and energy resources—whose privatization would require congressional approval.

This legislative proposal would direct proceeds from privatizations and liquidations, supplemented with contributions from the national treasury, toward the creation of a National Fund for Industrial Modernization. This fund would support the development of key industries with a strong regional influence, the reconversion of existing industries, labor training and retraining, and costs incurred through the privatization and liquidation process. BANADE would manage the fund, on instruction from the minister of the economy, who would also present an annual plan for action in collaboration with the minister of industry and foreign trade. The proposal also provides for a "privatizing supervisor" or "liquidation supervisor," as the case may be, whose functions correspond to the administrative and decision-making sections of the company.

According to the proposal, privatization could be implemented through any of the following options: sale of company assets as a unit or separately; sale of shares or blocks of shares in the social capital or productive enterprises in operation; lease for a given period with an option to purchase; and capitalization of debts (such as debt-equity swaps).

The leasing option is perhaps the weakest point of this proposal; the history of the relationship between Argentina's public and private sectors makes it desirable that there be no possibility to reverse decisions.

Privatization could be carried out under this proposal through bidding or auction (with or without a base price) or through the sale of shares on Argentina's stock markets. Finally, direct negotiations for transfer could take place under the following conditions: (1) when the buyers are the personnel of the company to be privatized, organized as a cooperative or through the Program of Shared Property; (2) when the purchaser is a cooperative of users of the services provided by the company to be privatized; (3) when the purchaser is a creditor who wants to capitalize his debts; or (4) when the bidding or auction without a base price attracts no bidders or reasonable offers.

If successful, the search for an ideal legal framework within which to transact privatizations will remove one of the past obstacles to the process.

An inhospitable investment environment. The Argentine economy registered triple-digit inflation in eleven of the thirteen years from 1977 through 1989 and verged on hyperinflation for most of this period. In a country with no prior history of persistent, high inflation, living with inflation has produced adaptive behavior and expectations, as well as economic policies and institutions, that would seem strange in other circumstances. Understanding inflation's effect on the economic environment of privatization is essential to understanding why so little privatization has occurred.

A fundamental characteristic of high inflation is that it reduces the time available for economic decisions. Strong oscillations in the inflation rate and the violent price fluctuations they produce also reduce the predictability of key variables and increase uncertainty. The terms for deposits in the financial system do not exceed seven to fourteen days, salaries are adjusted monthly, and fixed-installment purchase plans disappear. The conception of what is a normal or reasonable price becomes blurred. Periods of high real interest rates alternate with periods of sudden dissolution of debts ("stop-and-go" monetary policy). Years of currency overvaluation alternate with years of exaggerated undervaluation ("stop-and-go" exchange policy). In this environment, a capital market is only an illusion. The predominance of short-term decisions hinders credit arbitrage; variability in the nominal interest rate destroys any attempt at fixed-rate financing; and high interest rates prevent the financing of consumption.

Aggravating the virtual absence of a domestic capital market, the accumulated foreign debt and recurring doubts regarding its refinancing contribute to continued capital flight, since only a high return can cover the risk of holding assets in a weak currency. Producers face severe interest rate problems. Stagnation prevails and business opportunities grow fewer and more uncertain.

A feeble capital market, a weakened private sector, an indebted public sector, and a massive foreign debt constitute a fragile framework for any privatization process. Although the fiscal debt precipitates the need for privatization, the absence of a market for domestic capital, the stagnation of the private sector, and an undefined foreign debt situation all deter investment and undermine any privatization policy.

The combination of inflation and erratic anti-inflationary policies creates an economy that closes in on itself in the face of persistent foreign sector crises and a jumble of regulations. Government efforts to combat unemployment and recession—indiscriminate subsidies to sectors characterized by doubtful productivity, exaggerated and unjustified protectionism, and the purchase of expensive and poor quality goods—only reinforce this closure. Companies subsidized, protected, and contracted by the state are optimal from a microeconomic-level perspective, even if they are antieconomic on a macroeconomic level. Inevitably, sectoral interests demand that things remain as they are—preferring regulation, subsidies, and protection to transparency, deregulation, and competition.

These considerations constitute an obstacle to privatization that is as unyielding as the lack of a capital market, the weakness of the private sector, and the absence of investment. The reason is that economic liberalization, deregulation, and competition are three aspects of the same question: the reassignment of productive resources. Therefore, any resistance to transparency, deregulation, and competition is resistance to the privatization process.

Union opposition. The labor union movement is traditionally strong in Argentina. A high percentage of the work force is unionized, and union leaders occupy high positions in the executive and legislative branches. In the first three years of the Alfonsín administration, the Confederación General del Trabajo (CGT), an umbrella organization comprising most unions, was the main source of opposition to the government, replacing the Peronist party in the opposition role.

The most powerful union leaders belong, logically, to the economic sectors that previously enjoyed the benefits of an economic growth strategy based on protectionism, indiscriminate subsidies, and a strong state. If the current crisis calls for an immediate reallocation of resources, sectors that feel threatened will resist instinctively. Thus, unions tend to oppose any attempt at reform, including privatization. In the few recent privatization experiences, the unions generally played an opposition role throughout.

Only when under tremendous pressure will union leaders agree to negotiate—to avoid losing all their power. Such pressure is building in some state enterprises closely connected to the general public through the type of service they provide. Growing public protest over their inefficiency has intensified the pressure for change, leading the Argentine government to sign letters of intent to convert Aerolíneas Argentinas (the country's main airline, known for its tardiness and frequent strikes) and ENTEL (the state telecommunications monopoly, known for chronic defects in its telephone network and its inability to satisfy the demand for new phone lines) to mixed companies made up essentially of state capital.

Iberia Airlines of Spain signed a letter of intent to purchase a percentage of Aerolíneas Argentinas's stock offering, of which some will be sold to the company's employees.

In the case of ENTEL, a letter of intent was cosigned with Telefónica de España (Spain's mixed-enterprise telephone company) that would make ENTEL a partner in a new mixed, binational company. The "privatization" of ENTEL and Aerolíneas Argentinas would have been unthinkable only a short time ago, mostly because of union opposition. The powerful telephone union, however, has been forced to accede in a climate of public disgust with poor service and a critical need for solutions. Organized labor's attitude is now one of reticent support as it jockeys for a strong position in the face of privatization.

Nonprivatization and Petrochemicals

Argentina's petrochemical sector accounts for 3 percent of gross national product (GNP), or about US$2 billion. Some 65 percent of this production represents basic, derivative, and final petrochemical products produced in three "polos" or petrochemical complexes vertically integrated from the basic stage of production up. The remaining 35 percent comes from plants with a discontinuous vertical process and substantially higher production costs.

Argentina has an abundance of petrochemical raw materials (especially gas), which led the government to promote petrochemical development by supplying gas at very competitive prices. However, although gas's opportunity costs are close to zero, its overall costs, including exploration, extraction, and transportation, are quite high. Supply is highly concentrated as Argentina's petrochemical companies share the local market with no effective competition among them. These companies export more than US$300 million in petroleum products annually. There is also extensive state participation; state enterprises account for approximately 40 percent of petrochemical production.

Not only do state enterprises manufacture petrochemical products; two of them—YPF (Yacimientos Petrolíferos Fiscales) and Gas del

Estado—are also the exclusive suppliers of raw materials. YPF is the only supplier of virgin naphtha, and Gas del Estado is the exclusive supplier of ethane, butane, propane, and methane. Consequently, the state can set prices and ration inputs according to established quotas when supplies are scarce.

The state's pricing policy for petrochemical raw materials has had a major effect on the sector. The state has supplied the product sector at prices far below those set for raw materials used internally as fuel. Unfortunately, the succession of different administrations, the continuous renegotiations of contracts, and the establishment of special incentives have created a complex and irrational pricing structure for petrochemical inputs.

The local private sector manufactures 60 percent of petrochemical products, mainly derivatives and final products. It depends on the state for inputs, pricing, and incentives. Although the complex and changing "rules of the game" make the petrochemical industry unstable, this type of regulated sector offers clear benefits to the private sector producer. These benefits include cheap inputs, an assured input supply, and a near monopoly in the market that allows the state to manipulate demand through rationing.

Attempts to privatize the petrochemical sector center on the underexploited supply of natural gas, which should give petrochemical producers a considerable comparative advantage. State companies, mixed companies, and companies with highly efficient and profitable operations are the most attractive targets for privatization. The authorities clearly intend to move ahead with petrochemical privatizations. President Alfonsín's speech in December 1986 foreshadowed the dissemination one month later of the official list of petrochemical companies to be privatized, including Carboquímica, Atanor, Petroquímica Río, Petropol, Polisur, Monomeros Vinílicos, and Induclor. The companies share two common features: They operate profitably and with minor state participation. Efforts to privatize four of these companies—through the sale of state-owned shares—have employed public bidding and preferential sales to shareholders, with mixed results.

Experience to date demonstrates that privatization is not easy to achieve. Paradoxically, private shareholders themselves often delay privatization. For example, the Ragor Group, the major shareholder in Carboquímica, stressed the need for a law—as opposed to an executive decree—to implement the bidding for state shares in that company. Its arguments have postponed proceedings pending the court's decisions. The Indupa Group, major shareholder in Petropol, Induclor, and Monomeros Vinílicos, has filed a suit over the value assigned to its liabilities before privatization. The Ipako Group, major shareholder in Polisur, has continually questioned the decision to privatize, delaying the final outcome. Only the Bunge and Born Group, the major shareholder in Atanor and Petroquímica Río, accepted the particulars of the privatization decrees and the official price set for the state's shares, and only in this instance has privatization proceeded expeditiously.

The advantages of having a "passive" partner—that is, a minority shareholder such as the state who regulates the prices and quantities in the sector—are pressed home by official regulations that establish subsidized prices and quotas for scarce inputs. However, private firms' fears of having to match an international offer, or simply having to put up additional capital to purchase the state's shares, are additional barriers to privatization.

The petrochemicals case illustrates the complexities of privatization when there is no simultaneous deregulation of the sector. If a sector's survival depends on state regulation of prices and quotas, the private sector will not welcome a break in its alliance with the state unless it believes the rules of the game will not change. Clearly the answer lies not in privatization but in deregulation of the sector. In the case of petrochemicals, the government must define its sectoral strategy and answer the question, "What type of petrochemicals does Argentina want?" Petrochemicals are a compelling example of the need to link privatization to an economic growth strategy based on opening up domestic and foreign competition.

A New Beginning under Carlos Menem

The foundations for an effective process of privatization were laid within the first months of President Menem's administration. Although it is difficult to measure the success of these efforts at this early date, it appears that much has been achieved thus far. Yet opposition to the administration's privatization course is alive and well, particularly in labor unions and state-owned enterprises, as well as in political parties and in some large corporations that have profited from the state regulations.

Privatization efforts during the first six months of President Menem's administration can be classified as either basic or specific actions.

Basic actions. Basic actions included legal reforms, modification of government guidelines, and macroeconomic deregulation that paves the way for future sales of public assets. This action encompassed actual efforts to sell state-owned assets and corporations.

Two major reforms were approved during the first months of the new administration: the Economic Emergency Law and the Public Sector Reform Law. These two laws broaden the power of the executive in efforts to expedite reform. The Economic Emergency Law enables the executive branch to suspend subsidies and transfers that affect state-owned corporations. This process enforces equal treatment for domestic and foreign investors and creates conditions for a more efficient overall privatization process.

The Public Sector Reform Law is the cornerstone of privatization and is considered a legal masterpiece of Minister José Roberto Dromi. This reform declares a state of emergency for all public entities for one year, extendable for a second year, and suspends legal action against the state for two years. The law effectively empowers the president to modify the legal status of state entities and to create new entities through split-offs, mergers, closings, or transformations.

The Public Sector Reform Law also distinguishes between different types of privatizations: sales of assets or sales of shares, leases with or without purchase options, administration with or without purchase option, concession to exploit, and licensing. The law is designed to be flexible so that each case may be considered individually. It allows sales of firms to be total or partial and considers different transfer methods such as bid, tender, auction, shares auction (at the stock exchange), or direct deals. The law also achieves flexibility by permitting the assumption of liabilities by the state, tax benefits, capitalization of debt by domestic or external creditors, and foreign debt swapping.

The real revolution of the Public Sector Reform Law is that it enables the president, through the Ministry of Public Works, to complete the process of privatization without further approval from the Congress. The Congress is involved in the follow-up process, through a committee of six senators and six representatives.

There have been other official declarations made by the Menem administration, in addition to these basic laws. The administration favors privatization by deregulation and opening up the economy. The structural reforms instituted, however, will likely cause conflict with many private and public groups opposed to reform. Political, social, and economic factors may also obstruct the smooth transition to a more competitive economic environment.

The drive in the first five months of the administration to control inherited hyperinflation provided the impetus for nurturing privatization projects. The continued macroeconomic instability that reemerged in December 1989 and January 1990 created a new hurdle for these reforms. Paradoxically, the reforms require a stable economic environment in which investments will surge.

Specific actions. Specific actions can best be shown by enterprises that have undergone or are in the process of privatization.

ENTEL. ENTEL, the public telecommunications company, was slated by Decree No. 731/89 for privatization before June 28, 1990. The consulting firm Coopers & Lybrand prepared the strategy and administrative mechanisms as approved by the Intervenor, María Julia Alsogaray. Terms of the sale were established and several companies have entered the bidding process.

TV Channels 11 and 13. In December 1989 both television stations were sold to domestic investors, who paid between US$3.5 and US$5.0 million to operate them.

Giol. Giol is the largest winery in the country and was sold to Fecovita, a cooperative association of producers, by December 1989.

Highways. Final bidding is expected to determine which of thirty-three interested holdings will win the contract to conduct maintenance and repairs and the right to collect tolls on 9,800 kilometers of road.

Ferrocarriles Argentinos (FA). At the time of this writing, union opposition has delayed the bidding for the Argentine railways. Officially, it is said that the bidding will take place by late 1990.

Servicios Eléctricos del Gran Buenos Aires (SEGBA). The president decided to privatize SEGBA, a light and power company, based on its deficiency in rendering services. On September 29, 1989, the union and the government agreed on a preliminary scheme for privately selling 39 percent of the firm's shares, and awarded 10 percent to personnel.

Empresa Línea Marítimas Argentinas (ELMA). Bidding for sixteen vessels from this shipping company will occur in late 1990.

Aerolíneas Argentinas. The profit-making national airline is being sold; the whole process is expected to be completed in October 1990.

Assets owned or managed by the central bank. Action has been taken to speed up the legal processes needed to sell real estate, shares, credit, and other assets of the banks acquired during the past decade. To date, numerous buildings have been sold in public auctions. A new law is under study to facilitate selling of assets even before the legal procedures of a bankruptcy are concluded.

Oil reserves and YPF. The most radical reforms in the oil industry took place during the first few months of the Menem administration. Foreign and domestic investors were gradually allowed to compete in the exploration and exploitation of oil areas previously reserved for YPF. The reform allows exporters to maintain up to 70 percent of sales in hard currency, according to the decree signed at the end of 1989. The government announced that the industry would be totally liberalized by the end of 1990. This decree includes the reorganization of YPF and, more important, the deregulation of the related petrochemical industry. This move will make the privatization of many corporations in the industry attractive to private capital.

The conceptual aspects of privatization. Argentine privatization is a product of circumstances, not of adherence to a plan or ideological position. Although there has been no full airing of ideological positions, privatization has elicited both favorable and unfavorable opinions. In general, those favoring a transfer of state assets to the private sector have based their arguments on practical, not ideological, considerations. Members of the Radical administration who strongly supported the privatization process emphasized the state's incapacity to continue contributing resources to state enterprises. Thus, the fiscal crisis is one of the main forces compelling the sale of government assets—a desire not to contribute new resources to the national treasury but to reduce the expenditures required to sustain state companies. The fiscal crisis, in turn, is a by-product of the public foreign debt. It is not surprising, then, that "pragmatic" privatization coincides with problems with foreign creditors and pressures exerted by international organizations such as the World Bank and the International Monetary Fund.

To reiterate, the Argentine government's moves toward privatization in the past few years have not been based on arguments of efficiency, quality of service, or reallocation of productive resources, but on fiscal necessity. Within the framework of fiscal strangulation, it made no sense to support previously private companies that came under government control through receivership. They were transferred to the public sector to prevent massive layoffs. Little wonder, then, that unions are now the main opponents to privatization. Labor's interests often coincide with the interests of the bankrupt businessmen, since both benefit more from nationalization than from recourse to bankruptcy law. Moreover, state intervention is often legally flawed, allowing the previous owners of nationalized enterprise to initiate lawsuits against the state at a later time.

Only in 1989 did the Argentine government begin to promote privatization as the most efficient way to redistribute resources—as a complement, in effect, to economic liberalization and deregulation. Privatization contributes to greater efficiency because it leads to competition. Privatization of state companies or assets should not involve simply the transfer of a monopoly to private hands. The central justification for privatization over the long term will be the reallocation of resources.

Privatization and the foreign debt. The foreign debt has three links to the privatization process. First, the state's heavy interest load demands fiscal belt-tightening, which reinforces the need to jettison some state assets. Second, the debt engenders uncertainty—reflected in high interest rates and constant devaluations—regarding the evolution of these economies. In such an environment, it is difficult to find potential purchasers for public enterprises. Third, future arrangements will likely include more stringent conditions imposed by creditors on sales of assets through debt-equity swaps. In the end, the debt may both instigate privatizations and provide the mechanism needed to carry them out.

The relationship between cancellation of the foreign debt and privatization goes beyond the mechanism of debt-equity swaps. In Argentina, and to some degree in Venezuela and Mexico, acquisition of foreign debt was closely tied to capital flight. The private sector could buy foreign assets legally or illegally, because of the liquidity created by major public spending and state takeovers of bankrupt private companies. An enterprise about to be taken over by the state to avert its collapse would commonly increase its internal debt and send funds abroad just before its transfer to the government. This transfer of private funds abroad was facilitated by government liquidation of liabilities. That is, capital flight financed from abroad provoked an internal shift of resources from the public to the private sector.

The macroeconomic connection between privatization and the creation of foreign debt is the basis of the argument for retiring foreign debt through the sale of public assets. If the public foreign debt thus retired is paid for by sale of assets, inflationary expansion does not occur. The major limiting factor in debt-equity swaps, however, is the monetary expansion produced when public sector debt is retired and the assets sold are owned by the private sector. This creates an excess of private sector liquidity that must then be absorbed by the public sector at a high cost.

A dynamic privatization process depends on reaching a foreign debt agreement that brings real relief to indebted countries. The remaining obstacle in Argentina is the private sector's lack of interest. If relief were provided in the foreign sector, the risk of repudiation would disappear, and country risk would diminish. Correspondingly, domestic interest rates would fall and business opportunities in internationally competitive areas would rise, generating growth and investment. Within this framework, a massive transfer of government assets to the private sector would indeed be feasible.

Privatization and the redistribution of productive resources. The foreign debt crisis has exposed the exhaustion of Argentina's economic growth model based on import substitution through industrialization—adopted when the country's import costs outstripped the export earnings of Argentina's agricultural sector. When external difficulties persisted in the first half of the 1970s, the government promoted exports from these same industrial sectors, despite their history of overprotection and limited competitiveness in the international market. This strategy actually lowered Argentina's industrial competitiveness and increased its balance-of-payments deficit.

When the external debt reached critical proportions, the government saw the need to increase competitiveness. Doing so required a much more efficient distribution of productive resources. Thus we arrive at a more complete justification for privatization than those that cite fiscal difficulties or managerial inefficiency in the public sector. With privatization came deregulation and competition. Privatization without competition improves efficiency through private administration of monopolistic companies—to the benefit of owners but not the community. "Peripheral" privatizations often have negative effects since they establish a noncompetitive relationship between the new private company and the public one. Argentina's privatization experience in the liquid gas industry was negative because of an absence of competition and deregulation in the sector. Understood thus, privatization complements opening up the economy, and this in turn leads to a better distribution of productive resources.

Privatization in the Dominican Republic and Trinidad and Tobago

Privatization is increasingly recommended throughout the Caribbean basin as an alternative to inefficient and easily corruptible government-owned enterprises. Inefficiency in public sector enterprises contributes to the government's fiscal problems and wastes economic resources. Moreover, it increases private sector costs when it becomes a bottleneck for private sector activity.

Although in many cases privatization of state enterprises clearly contributes to increased productivity, it is not always feasible in practice and may not lead to improved social welfare. Small economies, like those of the Dominican Republic and Trinidad and Tobago, face particular policy design and implementation problems that relate to the small size of their markets, the personalized nature of economic relations, the special characteristics of their power structures and political systems, and the historical role of the government.

This chapter considers the possibilities for privatization in the Dominican Republic and Trinidad and Tobago, problems encountered, obstacles anticipated, and the probable effects of privatizing economic activities. A short survey of some of the most obvious candidates for privatization in these two countries indicates that firms would probably be better managed by the private sector, but that the transition to the private sector is not unobstructed.

Historically, public utilities and financial and other public institutions were often used to promote a Caribbean dictator's "private sector" interests and to maintain his firm political hold on the country. As concentrated authoritarian political power employed both private and public economic activities to further its goals, the distinction between the private and public sectors blurred. This chapter initially examines the current interaction between private and public economic activities and their relation to political authority and then reviews how economic policies are made and implemented in the Dominican Republic and Trinidad and Tobago today. The following discussion evaluates the susceptibility of public enterprises in these countries to privatization.

In the Dominican Republic the state owns a varied set of enterprises, including sugar refineries, manufacturing plants, hotels, and travel agencies, some of which are monopolies. As is frequently the case with public enterprises, those in the Dominican Republic have not been managed successfully. High production costs, inefficient production, the absence of sound and stable management, and the need for large government subsidies are recurring problems. In addition, the government's practice of developing public enterprises to obtain short-term political benefits has intensified managerial, financial, and economic problems.

Although Trinidad and Tobago has not had authoritarian regimes, the country does share many managerial, financial, and economic problems with the Dominican Republic. In addition, its major government-owned manufacturing enterprises suffer from a labor redundancy, an unskilled work force, and poor marketing techniques. Because many of Trinidad and Tobago's public enterprises produce manufactured goods, its public enterprises, like those of the Dominican Republic, demonstrate a strong susceptibility to privatization.

Yet privatization entails its own problems, as described in the final pages of this essay. Although privatization offers obvious advantages, the governments of the Dominican Republic and Trinidad and Tobago have yet to pursue this strategy energetically or effectively. In the Dominican Republic, state firms serve political purposes. Those that benefit from state control do not wish to relinquish their power. In addition, selling firms to the private sector would cause high unemployment, end the current cross-subsidization of inefficient firms, and openly recognize the socialization of a firm's debts. In some public industries, established land-reform programs impede all but partial privatization.

In Trinidad and Tobago, the problems are quite different. By managing land-tenure and land-use alternatives, the government hopes to cut output in the declining sugar industry, while simultaneously enticing people back to the rural sector to reverse the de-agriculturalization that followed the oil boom.

Finding solutions to the problems of privatizing public enterprises in both countries is no easy task. The short-term outlook for privatization is not good for political and bureaucratic reasons.

Private Sector–Public Sector Interactions

Dividing the economic enterprises in the Dominican Republic and Trinidad and Tobago into private and public sectors reveals a cooperative rather than confrontational relationship and fewer decision-making differences than one might expect. In both countries, the public and private sectors frequently make investment and pricing decisions jointly. This coordination results from their long histories of responding to the same political power.

In the Dominican Republic a tradition of authoritarian rule has influenced the market system's operation.[1] During long periods, important entrepreneurial activities were exercised as if they were privileges granted by executive power. Consequently, to be a successful entrepreneur during these administrations, one had to remain in the good graces of the dictator or see one's economic activities curtailed. In such an environment the major private entrepreneurs altered their behavior to respond to the perceived goals of dictatorial power. General Rafael Leónidas Trujillo Molina amassed a large fortune by coaxing entrepreneurs into making him a business partner on favorable terms, receiving portions of their assets as gifts, and so on. He then directed public utilities and enterprises to his private and political advantage.

The authoritarianism of the Trujillo era finds reflection in the presidential style and economic policy making of today's Dominican Republic. The presidency centralizes decision making and designs and administers the national budget. Furthermore, substantial budgetary resources are allocated to the discretionary "presidential fund" disbursed by the president directly. In years of budget surplus, the surplus is transferred to that fund, as are the profits from state-owned enterprises. Other economic policy decisions—such as tariff changes and restrictions on import goods—also fall to the president or to boards appointed by him.[2] Laws that determine economic policies tend to give broad discretionary power to the president, to boards appointed by him, and to other presidential appointees. For example, all the incentives granted under the industrial incentives laws must be approved on a case-by-case basis by the Industrial Development Board or the Dominican Export Promotion Council.

The former comprises five ranking government officials and five private sector representatives; the latter, only high-ranking government officials. Because these two decision-making units have broad guidelines, their application of the laws tends to be arbitrary and inconsistent. This personalized implementation of economic policy reflects a tradition in which granting privileges to the private sector is one of the government's principal activities.[3]

In Trinidad and Tobago the relationship between the private and public sectors differs from that in the Dominican Republic, but it too is conditioned by the distribution and exercise of government power. Before oil's domination of the Trinidad and Tobago economy, government economic policies centered on resolving labor shortages in the sugar industry in this rich but relatively underpopulated country.[4] Many slaves used in sugar cultivation escaped into the fertile uncolonized areas of Trinidad. After emancipation in the second half of the nineteenth century, many ex-slaves migrated from the sugar plantations to the cities and forests, generating further labor shortages. To supplement the available work force, the government sought immigrants from several sources and finally succeeded in bringing a substantial number of indentured servants from the Indian subcontinent, a practice that continued until 1920.

During the twentieth century, the developing oil industry enriched the state by providing large amounts of public funds in taxes. After independence in 1961, this wealth financed infrastructure development, subsidized health and education, and provided a safety net for much of the population. The oil booms of the 1970s reinforced the state's role with bountiful resources. In this country—with its history of slavery and servitude and "free" markets that had served foreign interests—the state's new role was to distribute the benefits of the boom to all social groups.

In Trinidad and Tobago, the massive investment required to develop the oil industry and other industries in which the country holds a comparative advantage exceeded the scope of the domestic private sector. Private development of these industries would have meant placing them in the hands of foreign transnational corporations, an unsavory prospect for a former colony.

Together these factors produced a large interventionist state in a very small country. The state's resources and enterprises and its willingness to interfere with the market mechanism have obliged the private sector to coordinate its investments and other decisions with those of the public sector simply to minimize risks. This has resulted in constant policy dialogues and extensive cooperation among private and public sector elites who, because of the country's small size and population, are often well known to one another.

Whereas in Trinidad and Tobago the relatively small private sector is dependent on the public sector because of size, in the Dominican Republic the private sector's dependence derives from the authoritarian nature of the government.

Candidates for Privatization in the Dominican Republic

In the Dominican Republic, state monopolies, such as electricity, are under government control because of distrust of private sector ownership. In strategic industries, a stoppage in a private enterprise could paralyze the country. The government owns other enterprises, however, whose acquisition was simply historical accident. Some were previously held by Trujillo and his close associates and were nationalized after the dictator's death in 1961. These enterprises include sugar refineries, manufacturing plants, hotels, and travel agencies. Labeled "the people's inheritance," these firms were grouped under two administrative institutions. The sugar plantations and refineries came under the State Sugar Council and the rest under the Dominican Corporation of State Enterprises. Unfortunately, these two enterprises, which had enriched Trujillo, soon became white elephants.[5]

The State Sugar Council. In 1986 plantations managed by the sugar council (Consejo Estatal del Azúcar, or CEA) encompassed 179,151 hectares. Of these, the 102,630 hectares planted in sugarcane constituted 54.6 percent of the area devoted to this crop in the Dominican Republic. But CEA was unable to manage these resources successfully, and its 1986 production costs exceeded those of the private sector by about 50 percent. Despite large government subsidies, deficits forced cutbacks in expenditures for land upkeep, refinery maintenance, and the like.[6]

A declining sugar market suggests that total sugar production should be reduced by substituting other crops for sugarcane and by eliminating less efficient growers. Although CEA is the least efficient of these, past government subsidies allowed CEA to survive, and its continued production actually forced more efficient private sector producers to reduce their output.[7]

Only in 1984 did CEA begin to cut sugar output and diversify production. By 1987 three refineries were closed and three more were closing, leaving six refineries still operating under CEA. Diversification projects developed by the private sector—including joint ventures and the lease of land to private operators—have increased production of fresh fruits, concentrates, and other crops. In 1987 CEA sought to redirect the use of between about 12,000 and 14,000 hectares of land previously devoted to sugarcane production. This may be too little, too late, however. The U.S. Agency for International Development estimates that a reduction of 48,000 hectares is needed to match sugar production to demand.[8] Although CEA has been willing to lease assets or establish joint ventures, it has no plans to sell any holdings to the private sector.

The Dominican Corporation of State Enterprises. The Dominican Corporation of State Enterprises (Corporación Dominicana de Empresas Estatales, or CORDE) was created in 1966 as an umbrella organization to administer and develop nationalized businesses. In 1987 this odd assortment of businesses—many of them assets of former dictator Trujillo—included seventeen manufacturing enterprises, two mines, an insurance company, the national airline, a real estate business, and a maintenance shop to service other CORDE enterprises. CORDE also administers some commercial businesses, including a car dealership and parts shop. CORDE's manufacturing enterprises produce cement, glass, paper, vegetable oils, shoes, tobacco, chocolate, nails, sacks and ropes, textiles, paints, milled grains, leather, and car batteries. CORDE also owns salt mines and refineries, and marble and plaster mines. In the past, it administered hotels, hardware stores, and even a disco.

The social-welfare justification for government ownership of this collection of enterprises is weak, despite the claim that Trujillo's "inheritance" belongs to the people and should remain in state hands. Most Dominican politicians oppose privatization of these enterprises on the grounds that it would create a negative political backlash. However, the few cases in which public enterprises have been privatized provide no evidence of such a backlash.

During the Trujillo era, the enterprises now under the CORDE umbrella were efficiently run and highly profitable. CORDE has had chronic administrative problems with them, however, despite several technical assistance programs financed by multilateral lending and bilateral aid institutions.[9]

CORDE's difficulties have multiple causes. First, the country had no experience in administering enterprises for social rather than private benefit before Trujillo's death and no managers who could run a state enterprise efficiently. Second, more recent administrations have failed to establish a soundly professional and stable administration in these enterprises. Politicians are frequently appointed where professional managers are needed, and short-term political goals edge out long-term aims.

The Dominican people ultimately bear the cost of these enterprises, which have suffered aggregate deficits for several years. The magnitude of these operating deficits is hard to determine, given the deficiencies in available information. CORDE's annual reports include summaries of the profit statements for its enterprises, but the data are incomplete. Furthermore, the published data frequently conflict with previously published figures. The 1985 report shows that Chocolatera Industrial lost RD$9,813 in 1985, while the 1986 report recorded its losses at RD$990,844. Sizable differences also emerge in data on the cement factory, the paper manufacturer, the insurance company, and the airline. The 1986 reports show CORDE's aggregate 1985 profits 13 percent less than reported for that same year in the 1985 report. In 1986, the chocolate, cement, nail and wire, glass, and textile factories, as well as the salt refinery, a tire recapping plant, the tanning plant, the spare parts store, the salt and plaster mines, the maintenance shop, and the airline all lost money. Moreover, they registered these deficits while the private sector was booming. Another shadow on official CORDE profit reports is cast by central bank data showing that in 1985 CORDE received transfers amounting to RD$19.4 million.

CORDE enterprises' administrative and financial practices have generally decapitalized them. Overstaffing, inflated payrolls, irregularities in purchases and product sales, and poor administration have produced large losses. The few businesses that turn a profit have frequently been decapitalized to subsidize other CORDE enterprises or to fatten the presidential fund, not coincidentally promoting the company manager's standing with the politicians.

One of the worst results of CORDE administration has been an almost total lack of maintenance, which provoked the partial or total closing of some operations. A large coastal hotel in a prime Santo Domingo location was boarded up for at least ten years before its sale to foreign investors in 1985. By 1987 CORDE's cement factory could no longer produce clinker and had to mix imported clinker with local products to obtain cement. The government has generally closed down or sold enterprises only when the financial burden has become overwhelming or when the lack of maintenance has rendered the enterprises inoperative. Trujillo's inheritance has been administered less as the patrimony of the Dominican people than as a bounty to be distributed among groups in power.[10]

Several government and CORDE managers attempted to correct the administrative defects in CORDE enterprises. Studies begun in 1982 reported excess employment in CORDE enterprises at 20–50 percent. CORDE's manager was prepared to lower these levels and hired a consulting firm to determine which enterprises should remain in the state's hands and which should be privatized.[11] His efforts to institutionalize the administrative changes failed, however, and CORDE's losses continued.

The Joaquín Balaguer government that took office in 1986 faced a tighter budget and worse fiscal problems than its predecessors. It appointed a new CORDE administration and instructed it to eliminate its operating losses. Curiously, the director appointed to CORDE was the former manager of the Trujillo farms, who came to CORDE after eliminating the paper plant's deficit by correcting irregularities in the sourcing system and firing excess workers. He took strong measures to improve CORDE's financial situation, well aware that these enterprises could not receive subsidies indefinitely. The state airline's deficit is so large that this enterprise is managed directly by the president, and not by CORDE. The cement factory is in a terrible state of disrepair and, although its total employment has been reduced to 400, it still shows an excess of 100–150 workers. Flour production continues to be subsidized to keep bread prices low, even though the grain mills should show profits since they obtain wheat at highly subsidized prices.

Despite the Balaguer administration's efforts to make these firms profitable, CORDE has no medium- or long-term plans to guarantee their financial stability, nor does it plan to sell them. On the contrary, responding to the high demand for cement in 1987 for large government-sponsored construction programs, CORDE considered establishing a new plant to expand cement production.

Despite its stated aim to improve management at CORDE, one can only doubt the government's ability to effect significant changes. In early 1988 CORDE's director was indicted and forced to resign after his son was identified as the biggest purchaser of controlled-price cement, which he then sold for huge profits on the black market. Such events do not bode well for CORDE's future efficiency.

The Dominican Electric Company. The Dominican Republic is exceptionally dependent on imported oil for its energy supply and is the only country in the region where such dependency has not decreased in recent years. The government-owned Dominican Electric Company (Corporación Dominicana de Electricidad, or CDE) controls the Dominican Republic's main power plants and enjoys a monopoly on sales to the private sector. Private companies also produce energy—mostly for their own use—but they can sell only to the CDE system. The large private producers include some sugar refineries and Falconbridge, the bauxite company.

Poor maintenance has caused a steady decline in electricity generated relative to nominal capacity. Before 1985 CDE's policy was to satisfy demand at almost any cost. Preventive maintenance needs were disregarded when maintenance would halt production, and routine maintenance was avoided since it meant a medium-term decline in output. An additional factor in the overall decline of hydroelectric capacity is the silting up of rivers that accompanies deforestation of the river basins.

Problems of energy production are compounded by distribution difficulties. Energy losses increased from 22 percent of the energy generated in 1970 to 38 percent in 1985 because of obsolete transmission lines, a shortage of usage meters, and lax administrative practices that allow electricity theft. A further problem lies in bill collection. At the end of December 1986, CDE's uncollected bills totaled RD$262.2 million, the equivalent of about six months' total billing. In 1987 CDE's revenues covered only 75 percent of the company's oil costs.

The inefficiencies and mismanagement particular to this sector are exacerbated by overstaffing, which by mid-1987 was estimated at about 50 percent of the payroll. Interestingly, CDE has tried to set the electricity price above the company's production costs. From 1980 on, it frequently increased real electricity price rates so that the prices charged commercial, industrial, and government users have formally exceeded average generation costs. This pricing policy was partly nullified by payment delinquencies.

Problems at CDE have made electricity service totally unreliable; there were 67,812 service outages between August 1986 and July 1987. Electricity shortages have generated serious bottlenecks in manufacturing and tourism development.[12] Not surprisingly, deficiencies in electricity service have provoked a dramatic increase in self-generation of electricity; every business that can afford it has installed its own generator. Estimates place current self-generated capacity at about 40 percent of CDE's effective capacity. The government has implicitly recognized CDE's inability to provide reliable service and the government's own difficulty in dealing with the problem. Executive Decree 1613, announced on March 6, 1986, requires any new business with energy needs exceeding 8,000 kilowatts per hour to provide its own energy facilities.

An indirect deleterious result of mismanagement at CDE is the inefficient privatization of electricity generation. The proliferation of small and inefficient business sector generators increases fuel imports and the capital costs of business. Worse still, the government insists on retaining its sales monopoly and has prohibited imports of larger generators that could be used cooperatively by businesses in areas such as the free zones and the Herrera Industrial Park in Santo Domingo.

Candidates for Privatization in Trinidad and Tobago

The Trinidad and Tobagan government owns the country's main manufacturing enterprises: the sugar industry, and the steel and petrochemical complex at Port Lisas.

Sugar. Trinidad and Tobago lost its comparative advantage in sugar when the once-prosperous sugar industry fell victim to the "Dutch disease" induced by the oil boom. The results were de-agriculturalization and the decline of manufacturing.[13] Because the depressed sugar market cannot support the relatively high wages prevailing in the domestic economy, sugar is a sunset industry that must be phased out. Nevertheless, sugar is the main source of jobs in the country and the industry employs an ethnically homogeneous (East Indian) and politically organized group, making it difficult for the government to let the industry collapse.[14] When the private sugar sector was in financial difficulty, the government stepped in and purchased the sugar producers. The government-owned company, Caroni, now controls the country's two sugar refineries and 73,000 acres planted in sugarcane. Caroni purchases additional sugarcane from small producers at supported prices.

According to Caroni management, the high costs in the sugar sector result from several factors. Perhaps the most important is the low productivity of the fields, which yield only twenty-two tons of cane per acre. This low yield reflects the lack of agricultural research and the concomitant unavailability of the new cane varieties. The variety currently cultivated was developed in 1944. The sugar refineries are old and inadequately maintained, leading to frequent breakdowns. Qualified engineers find more attractive opportunities in the growing oil, gas, and petrochemical complexes. Other production inefficiencies result in a high conversion ratio of twelve tons of cane to one of sugar. High salaries, a strong union, and labor redundancy—estimated at 10–15 percent of the work force—are obstacles to the sector's efficiency.

Caroni operated at a deficit of approximately TT$187 million in 1986, down from TT$350 million in 1982. Five years later, Caroni owed about TT$200 million to private sources and a very large, but unspecified, amount to the government.

In 1987 the company undertook a restructuring plan that featured product diversification—including a distillery, a dairy, sheep herds, and growing programs for rice, citrus, bananas, and pigeon peas. Only 33,000 acres remained in sugar. Caroni also researched the possibilities of developing peanuts, cassava, pineapple, fish and shrimp farming, and a plant whose residue could be used to produce particle board.

Caroni's labor problem is serious. The company has an excess of unskilled workers and labor shortages in several skilled categories. Given the sensitive employment situation, the company remains reluctant to cut its work force although it acknowledges its labor redundancy. Management, keenly aware of the problems, projects that its product diversification programs will cover operating costs and service its private debt within five years. Sugar production is expected to decline in response to decreased demand.

Capital-intensive and energy-intensive industries. When the Trinidad and Tobagan government realized that oil reserves were dwindling in the early 1970s, it decided to develop its abundant gas reserves to replace oil as generators of foreign exchange. At that time, energy scarcity seemed an enduring constraint in the world economy. Since energy prices were expected to remain very high, the government invested heavily in energy-intensive industries, despite the fact that they were also inherently capital-intensive users of fairly advanced technologies.

The original proposals to exploit the gas reserves included plants to produce urea, ammonia, methanol, liquefied gas, iron and steel, aluminum, and ceramics. In the petrochemical industries, gas would serve as feedstock, while in the others it was an energy source. Developing these industries presented special challenges to policy makers. The sums needed were quite large; moreover, external markets held the key to the industries' success since the technologies used required sophisticated labor skills.

Investments made in these industries were impressive. Most were concentrated in the Point Lisas complex, which now contains two twin ammonia plants, and the urea, methanol, and iron and steel plants. The liquified gas and aluminum projects were abandoned as too expensive and risky.

The methanol plant, owned wholly by the Trinidad and Tobago government, has a daily production capacity of 1,200 metric tons, all of which is exported to the United States and Western Europe. In operation since 1984, the methanol plant has proved the most successful investment in the Point Lisas industrial complex. Marketing methanol, however, involves high costs. These include the cost of bottlenecks in transportation. To sidestep transport bottlenecks, the company made a low-equity purchase of two special vessels. When energy prices fell and trade declined, an excess of world shipping capacity reduced freight charges substantially. With the high debt-equity ratio in its shipping operation, the company's transport costs were approximately 80 percent higher than available market rates.

Ammonia is produced in twin plants owned jointly by the government (51 percent) and Amoco (49 percent). Each plant has nameplate capacity of 1,044 metric tons per day. Ammonia production is physically integrated with the urea plant but is financially separated from the latter, wholly government-owned operation. Only 1 percent of the urea output is consumed locally; the bulk is exported to a variety of overseas markets. Together the plants employ four hundred workers, many of whom contribute to both production processes. The labor force is highly qualified but not unionized.

The ammonia investment decision was made in the late 1970s when many private investors considered it a risky venture. The two plants were bought from companies that had planned to install them in Calgary and Oklahoma but dropped the projects when market perspectives deteriorated. Because of the plants' high debt-equity ratio of about 4.5 and ammonia prices that settled well below the anticipated US$140 per ton,[15] the plants have accumulated debt of approximately US$240 million. The company has been unable to obtain US$25 million in new financing for a de-bottlenecking program that could increase capacity by about 10 percent.

The ammonia plants appear to be technically well run. Trinidadians have mastered the production process and demonstrated their ability to solve important technical problems, one of which required substituting sea water for fresh water in the cooling system. About 50 percent of the ammonia output goes to the urea plant as feedstock to produce about 534,000 tons of urea a year. Trinidadian ammonia is priced approximately 3 percent below international price levels. Given the difference in ownership in the ammonia and urea plants, price has been a point of contention. The government benefits from a low price, Amoco from a high one. Government officials argue that the urea plant's poor financial performance stems from its need to purchase ammonia. In other petrochemical complexes, ammonia and urea plants operate as single entities, shifting costs from one to the other, depending on ammonia and urea market conditions.

Problems at the ammonia and urea complex do not appear to be technological. The scale of operation is appropriate and the processes operate fairly well, but severe financial and marketing problems arise from the industry's capital intensiveness and market structure. Capital costs are very high relative to operating costs. Therefore, when product prices fall, plants with low debt-equity ratios can survive, while those with high ratios are in danger, even though they might have better technologies and be more efficient.

Since the petrochemicals production process uses products of some plants as inputs in others, and since some of these inputs are by-products that would otherwise be vented or flared, input prices vary substantially from producer to producer. Firms that are highly integrated, with internationally organized marketing systems, are better positioned during a recession than are independent small producers.

The main industrial user of gas as an energy source is the Iron and Steel Company of Trinidad and Tobago (ISCOTT), which was developed to take advantage of cheap energy costs. Because the country does not have a large supply of scrap metal, two direct reduction plants were built to produce approximately 900,000 tons per year of direct reduced sponge iron from iron oxide pellets imported from Brazil. Management claims to have a good conversion ratio to plain low-carbon steel and the ability to produce good quality rods, in part because of the low proportion of scrap metal used.

The reduction plant operates quite well. The melt shop, however, has had difficulties and the rolling mill's performance record is spotty. Management wants to expand the factory and install a new furnace at a cost of about US$5 million to produce higher quality steel.

Plant costs are high because of construction cost overruns, the company's initial debt burden, the depressed state of the world iron and steel industry, and the high price of iron oxide pellets compared with the scrap used by other plants. Labor costs account for only 11 percent of variable costs. ISCOTT's financial situation as of mid-1988 was critical; revenues were lower than production costs, even excluding debt service.

ISCOTT also has a serious marketing problem. Output is mainly for export to protected markets, but Trinidadians are not yet familiar with the intricacies of these markets. The major difficulty lies with production directed to the United States. Claiming that Trinidad and Tobago subsidizes its steel exports through unreasonably low energy prices, the United States slapped countervailing tariffs on Trinidad and Tobago's exports. After negotiation in October 1987, the Trinidad and Tobago and U.S. governments signed a voluntary restraint agreement limiting annual exports to 73,500 short tons. Given plant capacity, this industry must find other large markets if it is to survive. Among the Point Lisas plants, ISCOTT is clearly the most troubled.

Obstacles to Privatization in the Dominican Republic

The public enterprises that are strong candidates for privatization in the Dominican Republic are obvious. Most CORDE firms are located in manufacturing and commercial sectors where economies of scale are not particularly important. Many, in fact, compete with prosperous private sector firms. Yet, despite the obvious advantages of privatizing CORDE enterprises—and government-commissioned studies that suggest firms for divestiture—the government has not yet implemented a privatization program. Several reasons may explain this failure to act.

First, the firms meet political needs. Selling them would result in unemployment and tight internal controls, two things the bureaucracy wants to avoid. The government agreed to sell firms to the private sector in the past only when the plants or businesses had become inoperative.

Second, CORDE management can cross-subsidize inefficient firms with profits from the better-run—hence, more salable—ones. Were these to be sold, the need for transfers from the central government would increase and CORDE management performance would appear more ineffective. Further, because funds from sales would not necessarily funnel back to CORDE, management has no incentive to privatize.

Third, a serious privatization program requires the socialization of a firm's debts. Many firms have negative net equity; hence, to sell them, the government would have to assume the liabilities directly. Currently, the government assumes many of the operating losses and partially subsidizes the firms' operations. Open socialization of the firms' accumulated liabilities, even above the subsidies, would be a public recognition of the government's failure to run those businesses effectively. Socialization of the annual losses, however, preserves the illusion of the people's "inheritance" as something that could eventually produce a profit.

Privatization of sugar-industry assets is linked to land reform, itself a controversial issue. Possible alternative uses for these assets are clear: distribution as part of a land reform that could include small tracts; sales of parcels of different sizes to local entrepreneurs; government retention of large tracts; or sales of large tracts to foreign investors. Retention of title by the government would still allow leasing part or all of the land to local or foreign entrepreneurs. Partial privatization of former sugar lands has occurred through agreements with transnational corporations to produce and export to the U.S. market.[16] It is probable that more joint ventures with transnationals will be struck. Given the thinness of Dominican capital markets, it is unlikely that local entrepreneurs and capital can develop any project that requires large amounts of private financing, although this obviously does not preclude disposing of the land to local farmers in small or medium-sized parcels.

The government has not yet made a clear decision about the future of the former sugar lands. CEA's management is proceeding with a diversification program that includes some deals with transnationals, but it has failed to transfer these lands more broadly to local owners. Another issue in large sales of government assets is where to direct the funds so obtained. That proceeds from the sale of land and related assets would most likely revert to the central treasury could well be a disincentive for CEA's bureaucracy to promote a privatization program.

Any effort to privatize CDE (the electric company) would encounter a different set of problems. Declines in electric service could promote user organizations and generate political pressure for substantial reforms. Thus far, organized users are limited to small groups, and the solutions they suggest are far from comprehensive. For instance, free zone factories and others operating in industrial parks such as the Herrera Industrial Zone, could, if the law were changed, establish electric cooperatives to sell electricity to member-users. Electricity supply problems do not affect everyone equally, however, and this hinders user organization, particularly in a setting where personal relations are so important. Power outages are relatively costlier for the small and informal industrial producers who cannot afford to buy generators. Moreover, because they are more likely to be hooked up illegally to the CDE system, many in this group would not be interested in a solution that would force them to pay for electricity used.

Another obstacle to CDE's privatization lies in the size of the firm. To privatize it all at once might require a denationalization of its capital, a fact that could be exploited politically by an opposition party. A gradual sale of shares to local investors, therefore, might be preferable, with credit available to enable small investors to purchase shares on time. Here, as elsewhere, the need for government to assume most of the company's liabilities before a change of ownership further complicates privatization options, for in its present state the company is not likely to be attractive to potential investors.

In the absence of social agreement about solutions to parastatal problems, the most likely scenario in the Dominican Republic is that the government will continue to run large deficits in these firms. As in the past, drastic solutions will emerge only if things get really bad: if the macroeconomic situation deteriorates further, if real wages fall, and if inflation accelerates, along with exchange rate devaluation. Such changes would dispose the government to look for alternative solutions. A precondition—for either privatization or more efficient management of state-owned productive plants—is modernization of the state, a formidable task indeed.

Obstacles to Privatization in Trinidad and Tobago

Privatization problems in Trinidad and Tobago obviously differ from those in the Dominican Republic. First, the nationalization of the sugar industry saved an industry that would otherwise have quickly disappeared after oil changed the country's comparative advantage. When oil prices fell in the 1980s, the rural sector regained some comparative advantages, but the historic association of rural labor with servitude has blocked the return of manpower services to agriculture. The government's problem remains how to manage land-tenure and land-use alternatives so as to cut down on sugar output and entice people back to the rural sector. Privatization's role in this change is not simple.

In regard to Caroni, several alternatives are open to the government. One is to keep the company as a government enterprise and diversify its production. Another is to privatize the operation. The latter option would require decisions about the size of parcels to be sold, the provision of services such as credit and agricultural extension, and, if the crops are for export, the overseas marketing needed to make the operation successful.

Almost any solution for Caroni's problems requires that the government assume much of the company's debt. If Caroni continues as a public enterprise, an important policy question will be how large the government subsidy should be. The answer to this question and the fiscal crisis may force the government to take measures it would otherwise avoid.

The case of the energy-intensive industries is quite different. These enterprises cannot be privatized without foreign partners because the resources needed far exceed the wherewithal of the local private sector. Equally important, the export markets for these industries' production are already served by powerful transnational corporations (TNCs), likely to be more successful players than the Trinidad and Tobagan government. In this case, financial problems result not only from economic inefficiency, but also from a weak capital structure and lack of marketing channels and skills. To market jointly with a suitable TNC partner is an imperfect solution, since many TNCs use transfer pricing and it may be difficult to interpret the "market price" for a product. Conflicts like those found in the sale of ammonia to the urea plant can arise when different parts of the industry are owned by different parties or by the same parties in different proportion. It may be most feasible to sell the entire operation to parties whose relations can be adjudicated by market forces.

In Trinidad and Tobago, the problems that arise in dealing with TNCs are exacerbated by two factors. Recent colonial history has engendered attitudes that make it politically difficult for the government to deal with TNCs. Further, some potential partners are companies that have openly opposed or blocked Trinidad and Tobago exports. For example, several candidates for a partnership with ISCOTT are U.S.-based TNCs, which succeeded in having countervailing duties imposed on exports from Trinidad and Tobago.

Conclusions

A short survey of some of the most obvious candidates for privatization in the Dominican Republic and Trinidad and Tobago indicates that these firms would probably be better managed by the private sector, but the transition is full of obstacles. In some cases, privatization would result in social dislocations that governments tend to avoid whenever possible. Furthermore, the nature of the state in both countries, and of relations between the private and public sectors, determines the types of policies governments are willing to implement. Radical changes, such as privatizing an important part of the economy, are made only when the macroeconomic and fiscal situations are critical. In neither of these two small countries will the road to successful privatization be smooth.

CHAPTER 7

Toward Effective Privatization Strategies

It would be foolhardy to try to distill an optimal privatization strategy from the six cases included in this book, even were we to supplement the information base with material from other country studies. The problem is partly the nature of the policy process itself. Typically, policy makers from different countries differ on the priorities they assign various policy objectives, just as they are likely to hold different views on the effectiveness of particular policy instruments. They usually differ also in their perceptions of how economies interact. With growing international economic interdependence, expectations about the reactions of other country actors must be factored into decisions if policy makers are to foresee likely policy outcomes. The complications, however, extend into the very nature of the substantive field for which policy is being devised.

A good place to begin to illustrate the difficulties is to look at what privatization programs seek to reform. Some years ago, the *Economic Bulletin for Latin America* published a now classic article on Latin American public enterprises that attempted to evaluate their potential for development.[1] In that exercise, there was the hope of finding analytical regularities in a scene filled with empirical untidiness. The explanatory power of such concepts as market failure, strategic imbalances, intersectoral complementarities, and so on, did help to order the data, and more might have been done had later work on the political economy of bureaucracy been incorporated. Even so, a great deal was left unaccounted for. National petroleum companies, for example, now dominate that industry across the region, but the reasons for their creation and the timing of their establishment varied considerably from country to country, as have the results—sometimes dramatically.

One might be tempted to place a great deal of explanatory weight on differences in conditions under which the state enterprises originated, since these varied considerably— ranging from sharp confrontation and expropriation in Mexico to orderly, low-key negotiation and gradual transfer in Venezuela. Or one might give weight to timing, inasmuch as this, too, varied by a wide margin. The Argentine petroleum parastatal was set up in the early 1920s; Venezuela's, some forty years later. Yet neither the circumstances of birth nor longevity (with its presumption of greater opportunity for learning by doing) give us much to go on. If anything, the outcomes seem to bear out Thorstein Veblen's comments on the penalty of taking the lead.

Government-sponsored development finance institutions, established from the mid-1930s on, generally were set up in the belief that the market would not, if left to itself, adequately supply credit for designated merit uses. Nevertheless, public finance institutions, too, exhibit wide variation in efficacy from country to country and even within countries. Some, like Nacional Financiera of Mexico, Banco Nacional de Desenvolvimento Econômico e Social (BNDES) of Brazil, and Corporación de Fomento de la Producción (CORFO) of Chile, have performed in an exemplary manner. Others, such as Argentina's Banco Nacional de Desarrollo (BANADE), have enjoyed more modest success. And still others, some in countries where other parastatal financial institutions have worked well, have been failures, shot through with corruption or weakened by inept loan management, or both. Mexico is a case in point. There, where the Banco de México joins Nacional Financiera among institutions of the first rank, the Banco Nacional de Comercio Exterior (BANCOMEXT) appears to operate with reasonable effectiveness, though not with the élan and prestige of the first two, and the Banco Nacional de Crédito Ejidal (BANJIDAL) was fraught with problems for most of its life.

Even state-owned telephone companies, where technology would seem to constrain and structure managerial choice to a high degree, have manifested this cross-country variation. But the variation is unrelated to a country's general level of development. Empresa Brasileira de Telecomunicações (EMBRATEL), the Brazilian parastatal, appears to supply a level and quality of service that meets the needs of its customers with no more than the normal quota of complaints; Empresa Nacional de Telecomunicaciones (ENTEL) of Argentina is justly condemned for the miserable quality of its performance.

Privatization has likewise worked quite differently from country to country during the past decade or so, though the expectations that accompanied its placement on the policy docket were probably fairly uniform. Governments normally saw privatization as part of a larger policy package that included liberalization, rational pricing, fiscal and monetary discipline, and refocusing state efforts on priority activities.

Further, for all the talk about privatization and the professed interest in what it might achieve, what has actually been done to advance the process differs from country to country, as the studies in this volume make abundantly plain. Only one of the countries, for instance, has followed the process through to its logical conclusion. By transferring a very broad range of decisions on resource allocation to the market, Chile has, in effect, privatized major macroeconomic variables. The market sets interest rates, exchange rates, wages and salaries, and other prices, and even, since tariffs are now scarcely more than nominal, exchange ratios between internationally traded goods and nontraded goods.

Up to a point, the variation in privatization accomplishments may reflect prevailing circumstances or short-term trends—for example, the existence of overriding government and private sector priorities. Other items may rank higher on the state's policy agenda so that privatization is not promoted either aggressively or systematically. The return of civilian government to Argentina with President Raúl Alfonsín, for instance, brought with it no mention of continuing, let alone stepping up, the reprivatization carried out under the previous regime. The military government had spun off meat-packing plants, grain elevator companies, and a miscellany of manufacturing enterprises, mostly small and medium-sized, that had been picked up as part of the shareholding portfolios of government banks, principally the BANADE. Instead, dealing with a recalcitrant and disaffected military, bringing justice in the human rights area, and restraining and reforming a hostile labor movement claimed the full attention of the Alfonsín government—until rampant inflation could no longer be ignored.

The priorities of private investors hold equal value in the equation, suggesting the relevance of general institutional conditions as well as the immediate circumstances with which governments must deal. If other investments are judged more profitable and less problem-ridden, there will likely be only slight interest in the wares the privatization process puts up for sale. True, buyer interest is to some degree a function of price and terms of sale. But where industrial retrenchment has been under way for some time, and where the private sector itself has suffered decapitalization, putting a great deal of money up front to acquire parastatals may be seen as leaving investors too vulnerable to continued or renewed recession. Thus, there is little demand for the parastatals placed on the block. If, however, divestiture programs rely on generous credit (whether from the state or private financial intermediaries) to facilitate the transfer, this may simply recast the vulnerability in another mold. Chile's initial experience with privatization, which came crashing to a halt in the early 1980s, is instructive for countries like Mexico and Argentina, where adverse conditions of several years' duration have drained the private sector of much of its reserves and resilience.

The foregoing argues for a cautious recourse to comparative analysis. The subject of privatization is inherently comparative, involving at least implicit comparisons of public and private management. The country studies presented herein, however, point to the utility of a broader and more explicitly comparative framework. Contextual comparisons are called for, based on variations in circumstances, structures, institutions, and environment. What we shall undertake as a conclusion to this volume is a comparative analytic approach. That approach draws upon cross-country differences in context to develop a general orientation and guidelines for strategy alternatives, even if a formal policy model is beyond reach at this stage. For these purposes, it is helpful to look first at the conditions necessary for privatization to begin, and then at types of policy and sequencing strategies.

Organizing the Conditions for Privatization

Nowhere is there a clearer demonstration of the advantages of a comparative contextual analysis than in the exploration of factors that set the stage for successful privatization. Here the wide-angle lens of an interdisciplinary, contextual perspective is essential. While our ultimate aim is to focus on strategic alternatives for implementing privatization, and their results, we must widen our analytical net to catch factors that lie across or beyond customary disciplinary boundaries and yet make the difference between success and failure for privatization strategies.

Chief among these factors is the group with perhaps the most direct interest in resisting change—the functionaries of the parastatals themselves. These workers—white-collar employees, managers, directors, and associated professionals—have the most at stake, especially the upper echelons, who have been described as a "state bourgeoisie." A group satirized in Brazil as maharajas because of the extensive benefits and favors they enjoy, they are more significant than their numbers might suggest because of career and political connections and other ties with the central administrative bureaucracy. For the most part, the latter are inclined to share the same statist policy preferences, so that the core of the opposition to privatization comprises the legion of public employees in both the parastatal and public sectors, together with their kith and kin. According to most studies of Latin America's "middle sectors," this expanded constituency provides the mainstay of political support for the state's economic leadership. Indeed, in Mexico, this interest group constitutes a significant corporate unit in the structure of Mexico's ruling party.

Even where the party tie is less explicit, this public employee group often has an affinity for a particular part of the political spectrum, such as the Radical party in Argentina and pre-Pinochet Chile. Hence, party loyalties and party politics can be used to mobilize resistance through bureaucratic and legal maneuvering. This seems almost certainly to have been the case in the Mexican government's persisting coyness in speaking about "disincorporation" rather than privatization and in the Sarney and Alfonsín administrations' inability, or disinclination, to articulate coherent privatization programs in Brazil and Argentina, respectively. It appears to be an even more significant factor on the smaller political stage of the Dominican Republic and Trinidad and Tobago. Long-favored business suppliers, such as those who have profited from contracts with the Argentine Gas del Estado, can also be counted on to back these bureaucratic interests—a phenomenon often called "clientelism."

Three other institutional features of Latin America bear on this question. The first of these is the widespread unionization of public employees, which gives the group broad alliances with organized labor generally, especially at leadership levels in trade union federations. This organizational connection makes it relatively easy to play upon organized labor's long-standing preference for regulation and public ownership as a source of social benefits, and on its widespread anxiety that privatization would lead to industrial dislocation and massive layoffs.[2]

The second political multiplier stems from the centralized, urban-based political systems that dominate governance in most of Latin America. The antiprivatization constituency represents a much larger fraction of the educated urban electorate, particularly that located in the crucial metropolitan area of the capital city, than of the population as a whole. It is, moreover, a fraction that is strategically situated in relation to information flows and other sources of influence over public opinion, holding, as it were, an institutional megaphone for whipping up public doubts about privatization by invoking *raisons d'état*, national interest, even sovereignty.

The third feature, the very size of the public bureaucracy, likewise extends the range of influence of those resisting privatization. In most countries, national government employees include those working in the educational system, along with a lesser number of medical personnel. The Mexican teachers' union, for instance, is not only the largest in the country but also the largest labor organization in Latin America. Thus, the resistance movement potentially mobilizable by parastatal workers may be far larger than one might guess. Reducing the size of the federal bureaucracy was, for example, a relevant consideration in Chile's educational reform. Chilean educational reform not only decentralized the pre-university structure and placed it under the jurisdiction of local authorities, it also broke up the university system, regionalizing it somewhat after the fashion of state universities in the United States. Some have attributed this to admiration for U.S. educational organization, and so it may be. There is no doubt that the move has increased accountability and flexibility, while strengthening local participation in policy formation. The other side of the coin, however, is that the move also substantially reduced the ranks of federal employees.

Small wonder that this formidable phalanx of opposition should resist privatization launched in an economic environment bereft of job opportunities, adequate unemployment compensation, retraining, job counseling, and placement assistance. The economic anemia that intensifies the need for privatization is, thus, a major obstacle to its implementation. That privatization in most countries has moved at a snail's pace is altogether comprehensible. It is all the more significant, then, that the line of opposition has been breached here and there.

The obvious cases are Chile, Argentina, and Brazil, where for varying periods and with varying degrees of severity the routine political processes were put on hold. Removing the traditional political hurdles from 1973 to 1988 allowed Chile to move fastest and farthest in privatization and to take the lead in experimenting with forms and procedures. Particularly important was the mid-course correction made after the first phases revealed that enterprises had been sold too quickly, and with excessive use of credit, to large business groups, increasing the concentration of economic power and erecting a structure of business finance so shaky that it could not withstand economic reversals.

Interestingly, it was not concern for political opposition but the exigencies of sound macroeconomic management that led Chile to adopt many reforms that improved the political environment for privatization. Among the important innovations were the introduction of employee stock ownership programs based on the use of corporate reserves for severance indemnities, limitations on individual share holdings, concessionary credit with which small shareholders could acquire stock, privatization of the pension system, and the opening of public utilities to private capital to enrich the array of portfolio possibilities (in the form of more stable blue-chip holdings). These reforms contributed over time to a gradual "de-ideologization" of the process of privatization, which was increasingly seen as linked to capital formation, trade and development, and eventually, a resumption of growth in employment. It is significant, perhaps, that the CORFO office in charge of privatization is called the Office of Normalization.

In Argentina, the military government of 1976–1983 was able to initiate a wave of reprivatizations, more far-reaching in industry coverage than the successful privatization of urban transit in Buenos Aires in the 1960s, though most firms returned to the private sector were not large. There was some flirting with a more general program of economic reform, in which privatization would have been one of several measures to increase efficiency and enlarge the private sector's contribution to development. What was accomplished along this line was actually rather limited. There was some reduction of tariffs in the 1976–1978 period, from an average nominal level of 90 percent to 50 percent, but multiple exchange rates were retained for most of the 1976–1983 period, as were restrictions on capital movements, import permits, and exchange controls—including a state monopoly over the foreign exchange proceeds of export sales. There was little deregulation of prices, and almost no decontrol of public service rates. Before much could be done to reduce centralized decision making and refocus the work of the state on priority activities, however, the whole project was swamped by the ill-fated military venture in the South Atlantic.

For its part, Brazil suspended politics-as-usual for a longer period, stretching from 1963 to the political opening that began in the early 1980s. The interval lacked the severity of repression that characterized some phases of military rule in the Southern Cone, and there was much more continuing contact between policy makers and technocratic implementers on the one hand, and interest groups that composed the Brazilian polity on the other, leaving aside the organizations of the working class. In general, there was less emphasis on reprivatization and the formal privatization of state-initiated companies than on semi-privatization and, from the late 1970s on, improving the administration of the main parastatals. This simulated privatization was encouraged by a new Secretariat for Control of Public Enterprises. The secretariat sought by a variety of means to increase the commercial orientation of public enterprise, to remove barriers to competition, to raise managerial accountability, and to increase enterprise autonomy, especially in pricing policy. The last has proved to be the most difficult part of the process. Decontrol of prices for important state-produced outputs—

including gasoline and other petroleum products, electricity, steel, and telecommunications services—has in most cases been precluded by the top economic policy makers' stand on countering inflation. Moreover, some public enterprises, such as the nuclear power authority, remained impervious to attempts to install sound microeconomic management.

Clearly, one cannot extract from these cases the recommendation that civilian politics be thrown into the deep freeze simply to neutralize the opposition, but there are other features of the region's collective experience that offer more promising possibilities. The first is the importance of getting priorities right and beginning with reforms that provide a general framework for privatization. Those that seem especially important are liberalizing trade, as occurred in Chile and Mexico, and setting and maintaining a realistic exchange rate, with any deviation on the side of undervaluation. In addition, the public budget must be brought to heel by rapidly phasing out subsidies to public enterprises and decontrolling prices in general to provide more managerial autonomy. These broader measures, with their sweeping impact on resource allocation decisions throughout the economy, including the parastatals, are advantageous in three respects.

First, they eliminate a multitude of opportunities for economic rent and in so doing enhance the social acceptability of the whole economic package while simultaneously improving decisional efficiency. Surely this has been an element in the Mexican experience of the late 1980s, forming a basis for the social pact and giving the government leeway to open secondary petrochemicals to foreign investment. The subsidy element previously present in petroleum pricing would have made foreign participation much less palatable. General economic rectification seems to be the lesson from Chile's latest privatization phase as well. The continuing quarrels in Argentina and Brazil over distributive shares, however, seem inspired in no small part by the well-founded belief of workers that rent seeking and speculation have continued almost unabated.

Tactically, the bold approach would appear to stand at least as much chance as more piecemeal measures, if recent Latin American experience is a guide. The rapid adoption of these policies clearly places major adjustment costs on the shoulders of those most able to bear them and forces entrepreneurs into a scramble for survival that links accumulation with production virtuosity in contestable markets. The ability of Brazilian entrepreneurs to make considerable headway in international markets, the good showing of Mexican manufacturing exports, and the survival of much of Chilean industry—in the face of even greater dislocations than trade liberalization alone would have entailed—give hope. The outlook would be even brighter if Brazil's success in installing special policies to promote exports were more widely emulated.

Third, broad measures force parastatal managers to take a more commercial view of their operations. The reduction of access to subsidies, coupled with installation of better performance monitoring and evaluation systems as in Brazil and Chile, seems to impel public enterprise management to embrace a host of organizational changes that improve efficiency in the parastatal sector—provided, of course, that their hands do not remain tied in such matters as deployment of the labor force and pricing. Simulated privatization, consequently, enters the picture early as part of setting the conditions for a possible formal privatization later on.

There is little question that CORFO's success and the management of its parastatal subsidiaries in a setting of market forces paved the way for the Chilean program's exceptional achievements. The Brazilian record points in the same direction, though reconstruction of the general economic environment has not gone nearly so far. Yet, even though Brazilian efforts have been less comprehensive, in some respects they have been of longer duration. For example, government-owned electric power companies were forced as early as the mid-1960s to meet a kind of surrogate market test in their competition for financing.[3]

Significantly, even the Argentine military, when faced with firmer limits on what it could expect from the public treasury, took steps to stanch the parastatal drain on its budget by ridding itself of parastatals operated by its Fabricaciones Militares holding company. European experience would tend to confirm the importance of this stage-setting period, as would, in a looser way, the experience of Turkey.[4] Although in Turkey the actual progress of privatization has been as slow as any of the Latin American cases reported here, the Turgut Ozal government made real headway in subjecting state-owned enterprises to the competitive pressures of the market and altering their privileged status.

Apart from the direct effects of these general policy measures on firm-level efficiency, and the concomitant gains to society, the framework they lay down may be thought of as preparing the way for privatization by resolving the problem of labor redundancy and establishing greater financial discipline before the question of divestiture is even raised. Further, to put parastatals on a market footing the government has often had to relieve them of the burden of irremediable past mistakes by removing part of the accumulated debt burden from their books. Such a measure is justifiable when a new mode of management is in place; the liabilities result, in large measure, from defective policies that can be chalked up to the state itself. These state policies include the imposition of price controls, the use of public enterprises to provide unemployment relief or to channel subsidies to other groups (including the cross-subsidization of other state-owned firms), and reliance on inadequate performance monitoring systems. This kind of debt relief has thus been prerequisite for making many of the firms covered by our six country cases attractive to private investors.

Experience suggests that the helter-skelter financial situation of many parastatals, their huge accumulated debts, and their built-in labor problems are three of the most significant deterrents to divestiture. Hence, simulated privatization, whether through established parastatal management or through management contracts with outsiders, and semiprivatization, which taps the managerial expertise and financial backing of private enterprise, are a logical accompaniment to the sanitization of the macroeconomic environment.

The range of preconditions for privatization extends further. In most Latin American countries there is a great deal else that needs doing to improve the general policy framework. Better fiscal control over all government spending, stepped-up tax administration, a stronger capital market, measures to broaden the ownership of capital, the reduction of supernumeraries throughout the public administration, deregulation of prices, and the like are all part of the package for economic rehabilitation, irrespective of whether formal or outright privatization is being contemplated. They are also necessary to improve the economic outlook and restore the capital market to health—in other words, to enable the private sector to respond to opportunities offered by privatization and, incidentally, raise the amount the state might reasonably expect to garner from its divestitures. Again, the success of the later episode in Chilean privatization, contrasted with the problematic outcome of the first nine or ten years, seems to demonstrate the wisdom of this more measured approach. In any case, the record of the other countries, Turkey included, argues that there is no way to leapfrog the preconditions to hurry the process along.

Presumably, too, peripheral privatization—contracting out services or some operations of parastatals and other public sector institutions—would have a place in the preparatory phase, or even later. Drilling contracts, for example, have long been used by national petroleum companies to augment their own capacity in exploratory and developmental drilling—particularly the former where risks are higher. Some telephone services, such as mobile telephones and wireless transmission in outlying provinces, have been taken on by private companies in several cases. Argentina and Brazil have considered operating railway freight services and other parts of the total package of railway services as private undertakings utilizing rolling stock and tracks leased from the government. Curiously, there has been much less peripheral privatization throughout Latin America than one might expect, given that the subdivision of large-scale production operations into small components would presumably lower entry barriers substantially by decreasing the amount of start-up capital required and, in many cases, lowering somewhat the complexity of managerial coordination. Why more use has not been made of this means of increasing access in the economy, however, remains to be determined.

The evidence of what is required on the labor front is fragmentary and, hence, much less clear. Nonetheless, introducing innovations in parastatal administration to bring labor into consultation on organizational improvements, and measures to assist the relocation of workers to other parts of the job market as payroll reduction takes effect, seem essential. The Chileans have taken the lead in fostering employee stock ownership programs. The willingness of the Mexican government to transfer some of its parastatals to "social enterprises" owned by unions may well have aimed to mollify the labor movement in that country.

Meanwhile, limited though the evidence is, in certain fields characterized by a highly skilled labor force and dynamic prospects, parastatal functionaries may themselves take the initiative in seeking privatization. Such action may emerge from an awareness that their interests would be better served in the freedom of the market than by remaining in a troubled public sector. For example, the informatics software workers in a Chilean government agency that was destined for closure (so the government could purchase the necessary services in the market) appealed for permission to set up their own operation with funds from their retirement programs. Their request, which coincided with the policy objective of promoting popular capitalism, was approved. The resulting company, Empresa Chilena de Computación e Informática (ECOM), has done very well in competing for a share of the national market and in 1988 began to explore export possibilities as well.

It was also in 1988 that employees of Computadores e Sistemas Brasileiros, S.A. (COBRA), a Brazilian parastatal set up to promote national software capabilities, realized that they were falling behind in attracting and retaining talent. They, too, initiated a request (approved in due course) to take the company private—suggesting that public sector wage controls, justified on the grounds of fiscal austerity, may have an important impact by changing worker attitudes toward privatization. Meanwhile, in Argentina, a Peronist deputy introduced legislation to promote worker participation in privatization, and the 1989 platform of the Justicialists endorsed privatization for the first time.

This is, to be sure, a full plate. But it suggests that there is usually quite a bit to be done before privatization programs are pressed in any big way—leaving ample time to ready the policy instruments for implementing the program when conditions are ripe. Like happiness, it would appear, privatization is best sought not directly but indirectly through attending to other matters.

Sequencing Strategies

That the foregoing policy changes are needed to establish the preconditions for privatization should not be interpreted as suggesting that privatization must in every case await their completion. Far from it. Indeed, semiprivatization and simulated privatization (and, more doubtfully, peripheral privatization) are an integral part of the first phase, regardless of whether a decision is made subsequently to move on, in these firms, to formal or outright privatization. Mexico's experience, particularly in the reprivatization of shares acquired through the bank nationalization and the bold decision to close the historic Fundidora de Monterrey as unsalvageable, is instructive. These cases demonstrate that reprivatization may also become feasible before many environmental changes have been effected and that liquidations of the most hopeless cases can begin at any time, the sooner the better in order to stop the financial drain and to free resources for application to cases where improvements can be made.

The Brazilian, Argentine, and Chilean cases all reinforce the view that reprivatizations can readily get under way while preconditions are being put in place, though only in Chile has much been done to liquidate uneconomic enterprises. To be sure, circumstances forced Chile to reprivatize on a large scale, and it was the market that handled the liquidation during the ensuing period of rapid opening. Nonetheless, a significant beginning has been made in reprivatizing in Brazil and in Argentina. In Argentina, this began in a big way under the military government when the BANADE sold off many holdings, continuing with further sales of corporate shares from the portfolio of the same institution and from the Caja Nacional de Ahorro y Seguro in recent years.

Turning again to the Mexican experience, the privatization of the Presidente hotel chain shows that some transfers other than reprivatizations can also be included at an early date. In the preparatory phase, it may suffice for the government to invite investors to identify properties they would like to have put up for bids and organize the bidding to yield a transparent transfer with an adequate number of bids to protect the public interest. In at least three countries there is reason to believe that a few sound privatizations may be instigated by the employees of parastatals; thus, the door should probably be open at any time, with suitable supportive arrangements (but no long-term commitment to subsidize operations) for these to become commercial enterprises. The level of managerial and worker expertise is certainly high enough in more than a handful of companies for this to work out well, provided that the would-be buyers gain access to the necessary capital.

Finally, the contrasts among countries point to the pivotal role played by the lead institution in a privatization program. Where responsibility and accountability are dispersed—as in Mexico and, to a lesser extent, in Argentina—and where authority for implementation is not concentrated, it is all too easy for the process to be stalled by the interplay of intramural bureaucratic politics and confusion over priorities. These difficulties, coupled with a plethora of regulations emanating from different agencies, increase the transaction costs enormously and provide multiple opportunities for delay. In contrast, BNDES, the national development bank, has assumed de facto the leading implementation role in Brazil, managing the process for a series of three consecutive versions of an interministerial privatization council. BNDES put to work, and refined through experience, the impressive repertoire of organizational capabilities it had built up over the years as the government's chief investment banker. Further, it has called repeatedly on private sector firms to handle aspects of asset valuation, auditing and verification, feasibility studies, company reorganization, preparation of tenders, and securities marketing, as well as other needed complementary services. As the delegated principal for the state, BNDES has been able to maximize its working contacts throughout the business community—nationally, of course, but also internationally—and has been able to bring its marginal costs to very low levels.

Almost exactly the same description fits CORFO, which has served for years as the lead institution in Chile, first as the agent of an expanding state investment operation and, since 1974, as the pivotal agency in privatization. Both CORFO and BNDES have been adept in tapping into an international market for investment banking services. Both have been able to provide sound advice on needed reforms in the capital market, such as securities laws and public companies laws to afford minority stockholders greater protection and provide increased information on companies to the securities exchanges and the investing public. This is not to denigrate the role of the securities exchanges and their supervisory authorities in both cases, nor, in the Chilean case, the social security reform that brought additional investment expertise and pools of capital into the market in critical periods. But it is to suggest that without the additional impetus of corporate disclosure and other key changes, and without the expertise that BNDES and CORFO brought to bear, not least in the form of the professional respect the two institutions commanded, things would almost certainly have gone much less smoothly.

One of the most interesting aspects is how the two lead institutions have been able to capitalize on their accumulated expertise and reputations and, in some measure, hold at bay other executive branch agencies while winning the confidence of the legislature (in the Brazilian case). Whether this represents a sort of technocratic dispensation or has come about for other reasons remains to be determined. But the fact is that the institutional expedient has worked in both a large, complex economy with an impressive growth track record and a much smaller one that was struggling to establish a better basis for growth. An equally intriguing research question is why neither the Banco Nacional de Desarrollo in Argentina nor Nacional Financiera in Mexico has been able or allowed to perform an equivalent role in those countries.

Be that as it may, the combined experience of the six countries covered in this volume suggests that the possibilities for privatization have been gathering momentum, especially if we extend the concept to include simulated privatization and semiprivatization, along with formal privatization and reprivatization. The driving force in these cases is essentially structural, not political. The debt crisis may have provoked more discussion of privatization's desirability, but it has simultaneously reduced the capacity to privatize, at least in the short run. And political changes may well affect choices between different forms of privatization. It seems unlikely, however, that there can be any return to the policy framework that propelled the region into the industrial age in the four decades or so that followed 1930. Thanks in many ways to its very success, that framework has become outmoded—that is, afflicted with contradictions its designers would never have imagined.

Notes

1 William Glade, "The Contexts of Privatization"

1. For an earlier view of these privatizations, see William Glade, *State Shrinking: A Comparative Inquiry into Privatization* (Austin: Institute of Latin American Studies, University of Texas, 1986).

2. The administration of Carlos Menem moved quickly to start a new program of privatization, led by Arnaldo Musich, a president of the central bank. Although there have been early, hard-won legislative victories for the program, particularly in petroleum and telecommunications, it remains to be seen whether the internal opposition in the Justicialist party and the bureaucratic inertia discussed above will scuttle this latest effort.

3. The mystery surrounding the process of decision making was evident in the 1989 announcements of the intention to privatize the flag airline; the company that operates the largest mine in Mexico; and Telmex, the national phone company.

2 José Piñera and William Glade, "Privatization in Chile"

1. Editor's note: Although this may look like one of those "collective quotes" often lampooned in the *New Yorker* magazine, it must be kept in mind that published declarations of trade union leaders in Chile may reflect the

constrained situation in which the labor movement operated during the years of Pinochet's regime.

3   Oscar Humberto Vera Ferrer, "The Political Economy of Privatization in Mexico"

1. For a detailed description, see R. Villarreal, "La empresa pública en el desarrollo de México: mitos y realidades," *Empresa pública: problemas y desarrollo* 1, no. 1 (1986); and O. Vera, "El caso CONASUPO: una evaluación de los objetivos y logros de la paraestatal" (Monterrey, Mexico: Centro de Estudios en Economía y Educación, 1987), 85–87.

2. A. Carrillo and S. García, *Las empresas públicas en México* (Mexico City: Porrúa, 1983).

3. Ibid.

4. The original constitutional text, which has had over two hundred amendments, explicitly stated that the government should promote competition and avoid monopolies (both public and private) in all but a handful of activities.

5. R. Alvarez, "El Estado Mexicano y la empresa pública," in *Memoria del foro de consulta popular para la planeación de la empresa pública* (Mexico City: Instituto Nacional de Administración Pública [INAP], 1983); and J. Tamayo, "Las entidades paraestatales en México," *Investigación económica* 182 (1987).

6. Carrillo and García, *Las empresas públicas en México*.

7. H. Flores, *Teoría y práctica del desarrollo* (Mexico City: Fondo de Cultura Económica, 1972); Alvarez, "El Estado Mexicano y la empresa pública"; R. Ramírez, "Estado y empresas públicas en el desarrollo económico y social," in *Memoria del foro de consulta popular para la planeación de la empresa pública* (Mexico City: INAP, 1983); Carrillo and García, *Las empresas públicas en México*; and Villarreal, "La empresa pública en el desarrollo de México."

8. Carrillo and García, *Las empresas públicas en México*.

9. See S. Garcilita, "Racionalización y evaluación vs. privatización de las empresas públicas en México," *Empresa pública: problemas y desarrollo* 1, no. 2 (1986).

10. B. Rey Romay, *La ofensiva empresarial contra el Estado Mexicano* (Mexico City: Siglo XXI, 1987).

11. Carrillo and García, *Las empresas públicas en México*.

12. Ibid.

13. See, for example, Ramírez, "Estado y empresas públicas en el desarrollo económico y social"; Rey Romay, *La ofensiva empresarial contra el Estado Mexicano*; and Garcilita, "Racionalización y evaluación vs. privatización."

14. See note 4 above.

15. F. Calderón, "Preponerancia gubernamental y empresa pública," in *Memoria del foro de consulta popular para la planeación de la empresa pública* (Mexico City: INAP, 1983); and, generally, all private sector organizatons and their spokespeople.

16. Ramírez, "Estado y empresas públicas en el desarrollo económico y social"; Carrillo and García, *Las empresas públicas en México*; and J. González S., "Participación del Estado en la economía," in *Memoria del foro de consulta popular*.

17. Carrillo and García, *Las empresas públicas en México*, and Rey Romay, *La ofensiva empresarial contra el Estado Mexicano*, among others.

18. Miguel de la Madrid, *Quinto informe de gobierno* (Mexico City, 1987).

19. Secretaría de Programación y Presupuesto (SPP), *Coordinación general de modernización de la administración pública federal* (Mexico City: SPP, 1985); and Carrillo and García, *Las empresas públicas en México*.

20. I. Pichardo, federation general comptroller, *El Financiero*, July 14, 1988.

21. J. Flores, "Redimensionamiento del sector público," presentation to Reunión sobre Cambio Estructural y Su Impacto sobre los Objetivos del Desarrollo Económico, Mexico City, 1988. Other sources put the total at sixty-four, but there is no way to confirm either figure.

22. For example, according to the November 15, 1982, Official Decree, there were 106 entities in process of extinction or liquidation at that time.

23. Secretaría de Programación y Presupuesto, *Coordinación general de modernización de la administración pública federal*.

24. Some official documents include in this figure the cancellation of three projects and the resectorization (assignment to another government department) of ten enterprises. Obviously these should be excluded because they did not affect the government's actual size. See Villarreal, "La empresa pública en el desarrollo de México"; and J. Machado, W. Peres, and O. Delgado, "La estructura de la industria estatal," *Economía Mexicana* 7 (1985).

25. The disincorporation announcement was part of a spending reduction program, a detail most authors fail to mention.

26. Secretaría de Energía, Minas e Industria Paraestatal (SEMIP), *Reestructuración de la industria paraestatal* (Mexico City: SEMIP, 1985).

27. J. Machado and W. Peres, "Evaluación de la racionalización de la empresa pública," *Empresa pública: problemas y desarrollo* 1, no. 1 (1986).

28. See Electrometalúrgica de Veracruz, Barrenas de Acero y Aguces, and Oerlikon Italiana de México, among others.

29. Two such entities were Aceros Tourné and Industrial Azucarera San Pedro.

30. Secretaría de Programación y Presupuesto, *Informe sobre los criterios que fundamentan las medidas de desincorporación de entidades en 1988* (Mexico City, December 1988).

31. Ibid.

32. De la Madrid, *Sexto informe de gobierno*.

33. Carlos Salinas de Gortari, *Primer informe de gobierno* (Mexico City, 1989).

34. See Hugo García Blake, "Press Declaration," *El Financiero*, November 21, 1988 (the author was at the time chief economic adviser to the minister of finance); and G. Ortiz, "Mexico's been bitten by the privatization bug," *Wall Street Journal*, September 15, 1989 (the author is undersecretary of finance).

35. Secretaría de Programación y Presupuesto, *Informe sobre los criterios que fundamentan las medidas de desincorporación de entidades en 1988*.

36. Secretaría de la Presidencia, *Bases para el programa de reforma administrativa del poder ejecutivo federal, 1971–1976* (Mexico City: Secretaría de la Presidencia, 1972).

37. Ibid.

38. The National Development Plan annual review for 1987 argues strongly that "this process has *not* responded deliberately to privatization criteria." Secretaría de Programación y Presupuesto, *Plan nacional de desarrollo, 1983–1988: Informe de ejecución* (Mexico City: SPP, 1987), 132. For a representative position on this issue, see Garcilita, "Racionalización y evaluación vs. privatización."

39. See papers in INAP, *Memoria del foro de consulta popular para la planeación de la empresa pública* (Mexico City, 1983).

40. Carrillo and García, in *Las empresas públicas en México*, assert that 101 entities were disincorporated between 1977 and 1982. Unfortunately, these figures are not consistent with official figures published later.

41. In July 1986, the mininster of planning and budget officially declared that, "for the first time, a list was published of the priority enterprises the government will keep. Those remaining will be liquidated, sold . . . in an orderly way." Presidencia de la República, "Conferencia de prensa ofrecida por los licenciados Gustavo Petricioli, Secretario de Hacienda, y Carlos Salinas de Gortari, Secretario de Programación y Presupuesto," 1986. The list, however, was never published.

42. See, for example, Secretaría de Programación y Presupuesto, *Criterios generales de política económica para 1983* (Mexico City: SPP, 1982).

43. It is interesting to recall the work of socialist authors who recently stressed the need for fiscal discipline in government finances during the pretransition stage to *socialism*. See, for example, S. Griffith-Jones, *The Role of Finance in the Transition to Socialism* (Totowa, N.J.: Allanheld, Osmun and Co., 1981). If we stretch this argument, we can support precisely the opposite point of view.

44. M. Luna, "¿Hacia un corporativismo liberal? Los empresarios y el corporativismo," and G. Gaspar and L. Valdés, "Las desventuras recientes del bloque en el poder," both in *Estudios sociológicos*, 5, no. 5 (1987); and S. Sánchez, "¿Corporativismo o democracia?" *Revista vuelta* 136 (March 1988).

45. C. Garrido, E. Jacobo, and E. Quintana, "Crisis y poder en México: un ensayo de interpretación," *Estudios sociológicos* 5, no. 5 (1987); Luna, "¿Hacia un corporativismo liberal?"; and Gaspar and Valdés, "Las desventuras recientes del bloque en el poder."

46. J. Márquez, *La banca mexicana: septiembre de 1982–junio de 1985* (Mexico: Centro de Estudios Monetarios Latinoamericanos, 1986).

47. See, for example, the speech by the president of the Business Coordinating Council, "Palabras pronunciadas en el seminario anual de análisis del V Informe Presidencial, organizado por el ITAM," Mexico City, September 5, 1985.

48. Some authors have noted this possibility. See, for example, Luna, "¿Hacia un corporativismo liberal?" and Garrido, Jacobo, and Quintana, "Crisis y poder en México." However, we take issue with both. Luna's argument is that there is now a new "liberal corporativism," while Garrido, Jacobo, and Quint-

ana speak of new forms of negotiation between the ruling class and the big capitalists. Regarding Luna's argument, I assert that this is not a new corporativism, but a return to the same formula that worked so well in the past—"business as usual." Garrido, Jacobo, and Quintana fail to recognize the significance of the disincorporation process within their own framework.

49. This is why in recent years many government officials and labor leaders have had difficulty justifying many of the sales and liquidations of public entities.

50. The same can be said about the term "privatization," which is now openly used by public officials. For example, G. Ortiz, "Mexico's been bitten by the privatization bug."

51. Salinas de Gortari, *Primer informe de gobierno*.

52. L. Inostroza, "Las empresas paramunicipales en la actividad empresarial de los gobiernos locales," *Empresa pública: problemas y desarrollo* 1, no.1 (1986).

4 Rogério L. F. Werneck, "The Uneasy Steps toward Privatization in Brazil"

1. For a careful and forceful analysis of this point, see J. A. Kay and D. J. Thompson, "Privatization: A Policy in Search of a Rationale," *Economic Journal* 96 (March 1986).

2. See, for example, W. H. Buiter, "Measurement of Public Sector Deficit and Its Implication for Policy Evaluation and Design," International Monetary Fund, Staff Papers, Vol. 30 (Washington, D.C., June 1983); W. H. Buiter, "A Guide to Public Sector Debt and Deficits," *Economic Policy* 1 (November 1985); and R. Hemming and A. M. Mansoor, "Privatization and Public Enterprises," International Monetary Fund, Occasional Paper No. 56 (Washington, D.C., 1988).

3. See Buiter, "Measurement of Public Sector Deficit" and "A Guide to Public Sector Debt," as well as M. J. Boskin, "Federal Government Deficits: Some Myths and Realities," *American Economic Review* (May 1982); R. Eisner, "Which Government Deficits: Some Issues of Measurement and Their Implications," *American Economic Review* (May 1984); and R. Eisner and P. J. Pieper, "A New View of the Federal Debt and Budget Deficits," *American Economic Review* (March 1984). Werneck analyzes these points in connection with the Brazilian stabilization policy in the early 1980s; see R. L. F. Werneck, "A questão do controle da necessidade de financiamento das empresas estatais e o orçamento de dispêndios globais da SEST," *Pesquisa e planejamento econômico* 16, no. 2 (August 1986).

4. See Buiter, "Measurement of Public Sector Deficit" and "A Guide to Public Sector Debt."

5. That argument has been defended in Brazil by Mario H. Simonsen, planning and finance minister during the 1970s, whose views are inspired by the recent French privatization experience. See *Jornal do Brasil*, April 10, 1988.

6. This was lucidly pointed out by Adam Smith in *The Wealth of Nations* more than two centuries ago. See G. Yarrow, "Privatization in Theory and Practice," *Economic Policy* 2 (April 1986).

7. This point is well stressed by Yarrow, ibid. That it may be an important point in the Brazilian case is well illustrated by the statements of Mr. Nagi Hahas, said to be the largest private shareholder of Petróleo Brasileiro (PETROBRAS), the state-owned oil company. In an interview with *Jornal do Brasil* on March 27, 1988, he calls attention to the potential profit that stems from PETROBRAS's monopoly power.

8. For more details about Rangel's privatization argument, see I. Rangel, *Economia brasileira contemporanea* (São Paolo: Editora Bienal, 1987).

9. For a long time, Rangel has been seen as an important defender of an extensive role for public enterprises in the economy and was personally involved in the creation of both PETROBRAS and ELECTROBRAS in the 1950s and early 1960s.

10. For a clear-cut and striking recent case, see "Privatização garantirá expansão da Petroquímica União, diz Presidente," *Gazeta mercantil*, March 1, 1988.

11. Programa Nacional de Desburocratizacão, Decree No. 83740, July 18, 1979. For a brief review of the evolution of legislation on privatization from 1979 to 1986, see J. C. Mendes, "Uma análise do programa brasileiro de privatização," *Conjuntura econômica* (September 1987).

12. Programa Nacional de Desburocratização, Decree No. 86215, July 15, 1981.

13. Programa Nacional de Desburocratização, Decree No. 91991, November 28, 1985.

14. The loosely defined legal criteria for privatization selected three kinds of enterprises: (1) former private enterprises that had fallen under government control only because of financial difficulties; (2) public enterprises operating in sectors where private enterprises had already proven themselves able to conduct the activities that justified the creation of public enterprises; (3) subsidiaries of public enterprises that are not strictly needed to attain the parent company's central objectives and that are involved in unfair or unjustifiable competition with private enterprises.

15. Programa Nacional de Desburocratização, Decree No. 93606, November 21, 1986.

16. See Mendes, "Uma análise do programa brasileiro."

17. See Brazil, Conselho Interministerial de Privatição, Secretaría de Planejamento da Presidência da República, "Relatório de atividades desenvolvidas pelo Conselho Interministerial de Privatização, Exercício de 1987" (Brasilia, 1988, mimeo).

18. Nineteen different groups were allowed to participate, and the winning bid was 26.6 percent above the minimum price. The company was sold to the Cataguazes–Leopoldina Group, which has substantial holdings in public utilities, as well as in textile and telecommunication equipment industries. Interestingly, although it was not a stock exchange operation, the auction took place on the stock exchange premises for the sake of transparency. For more on Nova América's restructuring and privatization, see "Nova América: um exemplo de

operação bem sucedida," *Boletim ABAMEC* (Associacão Brasileira de Analistas de Mercado de Capitais), no. 6 (August 1987).

19. See "Pirantininga passa ao controle de Portland," ibid.

20. BNDES estimates that it has invested US$35 million in the company and plans to recover it through future sales of the remaining shares.

21. " . . . we want to underline an essential [guideline]. It is the efficiency criterion, understood in terms of the relationship between input quantities used . . . and output quantities obtained . . ." Translated from D. C. Moreira, *Programa de privatização: o grande desafio* (Brasilia: Conselho Interministerial de Privatização, Secretaría de Planejamento da Presidência da República, 1987).

22. See "Sibra é da Ferro Ligas," and "Paulista de Ferro Ligas assume o controle acionário da Sibra," *Gazeta mercantil*, April 12, 1988.

23. On the other hand, it is true that in certain extreme cases it has become difficult to ignore economic efficiency altogether. There is some evidence, for example, of concern within the Privatization Council about the monopoly power that could be exploited after the privatization of Caraíba Metais—owner of the only copper-smelting plant in the country. See the interview with David Moreira, the council's secretary at that time, published in *Senhor* magazine under the title "O Estado não desmancha no ar" in 1987.

24. For a good description of the procedures, see Moreira, *Programa de privatização*.

25. See "BNDES prepara privatização ou destavicão de oito empresas," *Gazeta mercantil*, January 27, 1988.

26. The enterprise's high profitability stems largely from the excellent productivity of its planted forests, which are capable of producing fifty-one cubic meters of wood per hectare per year—approximately ten times the ratio in Canada or Scandinavia. This kind of information has been provided in the official public announcement of Aracruz privatization in the press. See, for example, *Jornal do Brasil*, February 2, 1988.

27. A new shareholders' agreement established that BNDES will still retain some management authority in Aracruz after privatization. See "BNDES par ainda mantém poder," *Gazeta mercantil*, May 4, 1988.

28. See "Safra vence o leilao" and "Grupo Safra arremata acões da Aracruz por Cz$18.7 bilhões," *Gazeta mercantil*, May 4, 1988. See also "9 milhões do BNDES para o grupo Safra," *Gazeta mercantil*, May 10, 1988.

29. See "Celpag vendida ao grupo Votorantim" and "Votorantim vence leilão e paga US$72.7 milhões pela Celpag," *Gazeta mercantil*, May 10, 1988.

30. In early January 1988, David Moreira, the secretary of the Interministerial Privatization Council, resigned over the government's lack of commitment to the idea. See "David Moreira critica demora na privatização," *O Globo*, January 13, 1988.

31. Formally, the share would allow the state to have the final word on changes in the enterprise's stated objectives; pricing policy; investment policy; decisions concerning mergers, acquisitions, and the breaking up of the enterprise; dismissal of managers and members of the auditing board; and abolition of the golden share itself.

32. The new version may be found in "Nova versão do projeto exclui explicitamente monopóleo," *Gazeta mercantil*, April 14, 1988.

33. This happened, for example, in the privatizations of Máquinas Piratininga do Nordeste and Nova América.

34. See Kay and Thompson, "Privatization."

35. This was done, for example, in the case of SIBRA and will be done in the case of Aracruz. In both, shares constituting 5 percent of total equity capital have been put aside for sale to employees.

36. The importance of regional political opposition has been stressed by the former secretary of the Interministerial Privatization Council. See his interview in *Senhor* magazine.

37. See E. Bacha and R. L. F. Werneck, "Leading Issues in Public Sector Reform in Brazil" (Rio de Janeiro, 1988, mimeo).

38. The sharp increase in nonresidents' share in aggregate income in Brazil from the mid-1970s to the early 1980s was entirely accommodated by a corresponding reduction in the public sector's share. Although the public sector became responsible for the largest portion of the foreign debt, both the net tax burden and the real prices of goods and services produced by public enterprises fell significantly during the period. As a result, the accommodation of the swelling public sector debt service became particularly burdensome. See R. L. F. Werneck, "Poupança estatal, dívida externa e crise financeira do setor público," *Pesquisa e planejamento econômico* 16, no. 3 (December 1986). Also reprinted in R. L. F. Werneck, *Empresas estatais e política macroeconômica* (Rio de Janeiro: Editora Campus, 1987).

39. See R. L. F. Werneck, "Retomada do crescimento e esforço de poupança," *Pesquisa e planejamento econômico* 17 (April 1987).

40. Such difficulties were faced during the 1970s in many sectors. Common responses were to resort to large giveaways of public funds or to bring the firms under state control. See R. L. F. Werneck, "Public Sector Adjustment to External Shocks and Domestic Pressures in Brazil, 1970–85," Department of Economics, Catholic University of Rio de Janeiro, Discussion Paper No. 163 (1987).

41. See, for example, Moreira, *Programa de privatização.*

42. The legal basis for the adoption of that alternative strategy lies in the legislation submitted to Congress, mentioned above.

43. In a country with a population of 150 million, giveaways are no more defendable to 100,000 people than they are to five or even to one. As was pointed out by Brittan: "Cheap disposal price is a regressive subsidy from the general body of tax payers to those on the fringes of the existing shareholder class." He was referring to the British case, in light of its less equitable distribution of both income and wealth. See S. Brittan, "Privatization: A Comment on Kay and Thompson," *Economic Journal* 96 (March 1986).

44. Paulo Aragão, a corporate lawyer, stressed this point before the Privatization Council.

45. See D. Carneiro and R. Werneck, "Managing Brazil's External Debt: The Contribution of Debt Reduction Schemes" (Rio de Janeiro, July 1988, mimeo).

5   Javier A. González Fraga, "Argentine Privatization in Retrospect"

1. Information for this chapter was compiled in May 1988.

6   Francisco E. Thoumi, "Privatization in the Dominican Republic and Trinidad and Tobago"

1. Authoritarianism and extreme power concentration in the presidency characterize the Dominican Republic's political system. See H. J. Wiarda and M. J. Kryzanek, *The Dominican Republic: A Caribbean Crucible* (Boulder, Colo.: Westview, 1982), chaps. 3, 4, and 7.

2. Privileges such as tariff exonerations and licenses to import cars have frequently been dispensed on a case-by-case basis by the president personally. This was done liberally during the last months of the Jorge-Blanco regime. See J. Hartlyn, "The Dominican Republic," *Latin American and Caribbean Contemporary Record, Volume VI 1986–1987*, ed. A. F. Lowenthal (New Haven: Holmes and Meier, forthcoming).

3. It is not a coincidence that Trujillo's favorite title was "benefactor," which reflects the paternalistic and authoritarian nature of his tenure.

4. The literature on this topic is extensive. A good short history of Trinidad is B. Bereton, *A History of Modern Trinidad 1783–1962* (London: Heinemann Education Books, 1981).

5. Problems and mismanagement of the state enterprises in the Dominican Republic have a long history. As early as 1971, Warren J. Bilkey pointed out the weaknesses and corruption in both CEA and CORDE. His work did not mention these institutions or the Dominican Republic by name, though "for fear of personal reprisal." See W. J. Bilkey, "Public Enterprise Models and a Caribbean Experience," *Inter-American Economic Affairs* 25, no. 3 (Winter 1971), p. 43.

6. Government subsidies were RD$26.3 million in 1985 and RD$86.9 million in 1986.

7. Two of the three mills belonging to a private producer were closed because of this. See World Bank, *Dominican Republic: An Agenda for Reform* (1987).

8. See U.S. Foreign Agricultural Service, "Dominican Republic: Annual Agricultural Situation Report," DR-7008, (Washington, D.C.: USFAS, 1987, mimeo).

9. The World Bank and the Inter-American Development Bank have provided monetary assistance. See the AID-financed Asociación de Desarrollo Económico de Latinoamérica, "Análisis general de las empresas manufactureras del estado bajo la administración de CORDE," Report to the Industrial Development Corporation, October 1967. Bilkey argues that these technical assistance programs often fail because the consultants tend to take at face value the erroneous data provided by the firm. See Bilkey, "Public Enterprise Models."

10. Bilkey proposes a "Mafia" model to explain this behavior. He sketches his model as follows:

> Assume: The government is the sole owner of a monopolistic manu-facturing enterprise that is protected from foreign competition by high import access to both the subsidies and the gross revenues of that enter-prise, but do not know how long they can continue that privilege. They treat those revenues as their personal preserve, and will resort to vio-lence to keep their prerogatives. . . . The government funds milked off by the powerful group are incorrectly reported in the enterprise's account. Then: No outside analyst (outside that powerful group) will be given records showing the enterprise's true situation. Since he will be given fictitious data, his analysis of the enterprise's situation probably will be erroneous. . . . The powerful group milking the enterprise would have little incentive to improve the enterprise's long-run performance. The primary concern would be to get as much for themselves as possible; this would require a manager who cooperates with them, plus maximum short-run gross earnings and maximum short-run government subsi-dies. They also would fight to maintain the enterprise's position in the market (including the elimination of competitors), and to keep a friendly government in power. Where the Mafia model applies, improving the public enterprise's efficiency (in the narrow technical sense of that term) would do nothing to improve the social well-being of that country. In-stead, it would increase the income (therefore to some extent the political power) of those who are milking it. To improve the social well-being of the people of that country, first priority should be given to eliminating the powerful group's hold on the enterprise. Once that is accomplished, it probably would be socially worthwhile to help improve the enterprise's performance.

Bilkey, "Public Enterprise Models," pp. 42–44. Bilkey also describes an alternative model proposed by an "older provincial businessman" based on the concept of "the bottle," slang for getting something without earning it. A use-lessly employed individual is referred to as having a "bottle." Interestingly, one of the largest buildings in Santo Domingo, built to house several government ministries and offices, is popularly called the *huacal*, a wooden crate used to transport beer and soda bottles. A newer and smaller building nearby, built to house an overflowing bureaucracy, is known as the *huacalito*.

11. CORDE's manager in 1987 was unaware of such a study, and copies were not available.

12. In 1987 President Balaguer established a commission to evaluate CDE and recommend solutions to its problems. See *Evaluación de la situación actual de la Corporación Dominicana de Electricidad y recomendaciones* (Santiago: CDE, May 1987).

13. H. S. Pollard, "The Erosion of Agriculture in an Oil Economy: The Case of Export Crop Production in Trinidad," *World Development* 13, no. 7 (1985), pp. 819–35. Furthermore the 1982 Agricultural Census shows that abandoned crop lands were 13.3 percent of the land under grass and crop cultivation that year. Food imports have grown in importance so that in 1986 they represented 23.9 percent of total merchandise imports. The decline in manufacturing is discussed

in F. Thoumi, "Long-term Industrialization Trends in Two Small Caribbean Countries: The Cases of the Dominican Republic and Trinidad and Tobago" (Presentation at the XIV International Congress of the Latin American Studies Association, New Orleans, March 17–19, 1988).

14. Caroni estimates that the sugar industry supports 15 percent of the country's population.

15. For example, the fourth-quarter 1986 price was only about US$78 per ton.

16. An example is the deal with Dole to produce, can, and export pineapples.

7   William Glade, "Toward Effective Privatization Strategies"

1. "Public Enterprises: Their Present Significance and Their Potential in Development," *Economic Bulletin for Latin America* 16, no. 1 (1971), pp. 1–70

2. See Peter Accolla, *Caught in the Middle: A Special Study of Privatization in Latin America and Its Impact on Workers and Their Unions* (Washington, D.C.: U.S. Department of Labor, Bureau of International Labor Affairs, November 1988).

3. See Judith Tendler, *Electric Power in Brazil* (Cambridge, Mass.: Harvard University Press, 1968).

4. Vincent Wright and John Vickers, "The Politics of Industrial Privatization in Western Europe: An Overview"; Joaquim Silvestre, "Privatization in Spain"; and Roger S. Leeds, "Turkey: Implementation of a Privatization Strategy" (Presentations at the conference on Privatization of Public Enterprises in Latin America, cosponsored by the Institute of the Americas, the Center for U.S.–Mexican Studies, and the Center for Iberian and Latin American Studies, University of California, San Diego, La Jolla, California, May 2–4, 1988).

About the Contributors

William Glade is associate director of the United States Information Agency in charge of the Bureau of Educational and Cultural Affairs. He was confirmed on October 7, 1989. Before that, he served as acting secretary of the Latin American Program of the Woodrow Wilson International Center for Scholars in the Smithsonian Institution, where he was also a senior program associate. Glade is on leave from his position as professor of economics with the University of Texas at Austin, a position he has held since 1970. From 1971 to 1986, he directed that university's Institute of Latin American Studies, except for a sabbatical in 1982, when he was Mellon Visiting Scholar at the University of California, Los Angeles.

Before joining the faculty of the University of Texas, Glade was professor of business and economics at the University of Wisconsin, Madison, where he had been a member of the faculty and active in the Ibero-American Studies Program since 1960. While at Wisconsin, he also directed the Center for International Business Research. He began his teaching career at the University of Maryland's Economics Department in 1957.

Javier A. González Fraga has since June 1990 been president of the central bank of Argentina, a position he also held from July to November 1989. Previously he advised numerous financial and industrial companies, including major international banks. He has also written several books on capital markets and privatization.

José Piñera is chairman of José Piñera y Asociados, a consulting firm in the field of economics, finance, and political analysis. He is a member of the team of economists that has transformed the Chilean economy. As minister of labor and social security (1979–1980) he was the architect of the privatization of the Chilean pension system and of the new trade union code. As minister of mining, he wrote the new Chilean mining legislation. Piñera is a member of the International Finance Corporation Business Advisory Council and is on the board of several corporations.

Francisco E. Thoumi is a professor of economics at California State University, Chico. He was formerly with the Inter-American Development Bank and has also been an economist for the World Bank and a division chief at the National Planning Department of Colombia. Thoumi has taught at several Washington, D.C., area universities and has done extensive research on industrialization, international and intraregional trade in Latin America, and institutional aspects of development.

Oscar Humberto Vera Ferrer is currently deputy director for economic studies for Grupo DESC. Vera was deputy director of economic analysis in Mexico's Ministry of Planning and Budget and director of macroeconomic analysis at the Ministry of Energy, Mining, and Parastatal Industries. He is also a part-time professor of economics for the Instituto Tecnológico Autónomo de México (ITAM). Vera has published extensively on economic issues in Mexico.

Rogério L. F. Werneck holds a Ph.D. from Harvard University and is a professor in the Department of Economics of the Catholic University of Rio de Janeiro, a department he headed for the first half of the 1980s. His publications have concentrated on the analysis of the Brazilian public sector in relation to stabilization policy and economic growth prospects in the country.

Index